D0850484

*The Reason, the Understanding, and Time*

*The Reason*

*the Understanding*

*and Time*

ARTHUR O. LOVEJOY

*Baltimore: The Johns Hopkins Press*

Distributed in Great Britain by Oxford University Press, London

Printed in the United States of America

by The Haddon Craftsmen, Scranton, Pa.

Library of Congress Catalog Card Number 61–8177

This book has been brought to publication with the
assistance of a grant from The Ford Foundation.

# Contents

# *Preface*

Some readers of this book may perhaps be puzzled by finding that many of the philosophers often referred to by historians of philosophy as "Romanticists" are not here so designated. There are several reasons for this omission. First, Jacobi and Schelling, two of the philosophers dealt with most extensively in this volume, never, so far as I know, applied the terms "Romantic" or "Romanticism" either to themselves or to their own doctrines. Second, with the exception of the Greek *physis* and its derivatives, and the Latin *natura* and its derivatives in modern languages, there are few words current among Western peoples which manifest a higher degree of what may be called semantic fecundity than "Romantic" or "Romanticism." The prodigious number of senses, often conflicting senses, attached to *natura* and its derivatives I have pointed out in the appendix to *Primitivism and Related Ideas in Antiquity.*[1] *Physis*

[1] Baltimore, 1935.

and *natura,* however, are very old words. They have figured in the vocabulary of philosophers for more than two thousand years. But the adjective "Romantic" and the noun "Romanticism" as designations of a philosophical school, doctrine, or tendency are relatively new words. They first began to play a role in philosophical treatises and discussions only in the last decade of the eighteenth century and in the beginning of the nineteenth. The terms were initially used in a definite sense by the Schlegels, who at the outset were chiefly preoccupied with two peculiar problems:

(a) What are the essential and distinguishing characteristics of classical, *i.e.,* Greek, art and thought and culture, on the one hand, and of non-classical, *i.e.,* modern art, etc., on the other? (b) How are these differences to be explained historically? They began their reflection on these problems while still assuming the superiority of the 'classical'; their lucubrations on the subject are an episode in the history of the quarrel over the Ancients and Moderns. Now their answer to the second question was that the fundamental differences between classical and 'modern' ways of thinking must be due to one or both of the two great historic events which brought the ancient culture to an end: the introduction of Christianity and the invasions of the Nordic or Germanic peoples. This suggested to them, in part, the answer to their other question. If you want to know, in terms of basic ideas—of preconceptions, valuations, or emotional suscepti- bilities—what distinguishes the classical from the modern or 'Romantic,' you have but to determine wherein the Christian view of life or of the universe fundamentally differs from the Greek, or the Ger- manic or Nordic from the Latin or Mediterranean. At first they (certainly Friedrich Schlegel) con- ceived the former, at least, to be a difference for the worse. But in their attempt—much influenced by Schiller's essay [*Ueber naive und sentimen- talische Dichtung*] . . . to formulate the 'essence' of the 'modern' or Christian *Lebensanschauung*, they came . . . to find this in certain propensities or assumptions such as the craving . . . for infinite values or infinite objects for thought or imagination to contemplate, or for the will to aim at, a love of mystery, otherworldliness, an awareness of the duality of man's constitution, a preoccupation with the inner life, and a sense of man's inner corrup- tion—all of these being contrasted with the classical sense for 'form' and limits, the supposed Greek love of clarity, absorption in the beauty of this world, 'objectivity' (*i.e.*, looking out and not in), untroubled unity of personality, and 'serenity.' And some, at least, of the former propensities or as- sumptions these writers found congenial to their own imaginations or temperaments; and they there- upon abruptly turned from what they conceived (with a good deal of historical error) to be the classical mode of art and thought to its opposite, which they had already named 'Romantic.'[2]

Although one can determine fairly well how the terms were used initially, they soon came to be employed in so many other and such various senses that no lexicographer has ever come near to enumerating them correctly and exhaustively. The amazing diversity of meanings I have already attempted to exhibit—though the list is incomplete—in the article "On the Discrimination of Romanticisms."[3] I think this article furnishes sufficient proof, if any were needed, that "Romanticism" now has no generally understood meaning and has therefore come to be useless as a verbal symbol. And if I may repeat a plea made in an earlier writing: few things are more needful for historians of ideas than to get rid of the logical confusions associated with this linguistically extraordinary word "Romanticism" and, in fact, to cease asking, "What *is* Romanticism?"

[2] I quote this brief account of the early use of these conceptions from my article "The Meaning of Romanticism for the Historian of Ideas," *Journal of the History of Ideas*, June, 1941, pp. 266-67. For a more extensive treatment of the history of these same conceptions *cf.* "The Meaning of 'Romantic' in Early German Romanticism" and "Schiller and the Genesis of German Romanticism" in *Essays in the History of Ideas* (Baltimore, 1948).

[3] In *Essays in the History of Ideas* (Baltimore, 1948).

For an answer to it, whether expressed or implied, will either (a) contain the factually false assumption . . . that the word has one understood and accepted meaning, or else (b) it will be a personal definition of the word conveying no information except about the definer's private taste in terminology, and is not open to discussion, or comparison with any objective matters of fact—since personal preferences in the definition of terms are not discussable, provided the definitions are not self-contradictory. Yet those who propound definitions—new or old—of 'Romanticism,' appear usually to suppose that they are *not* merely uttering a verbal proposition—a statement of the signification which they choose to attach to a term—but are putting forth a proposition of historical fact, capable of discussion and verification. This singular confusion in most instances can be seen to rest upon a vague, tacit assumption that there is a kind of determinate entity existing prior to the definition, an object or an essence, or Platonic Idea—which *must* be the thing that the word 'Romantic' or 'Romanticism' denotes, but which, when it is discovered, must then be assumed to be exemplified or embodied in all the writers or writings which have been conventionally called, or which the particular historian or critic is accustomed to call, 'Romantic.' In determining what this Romantic essence is, the inquirer is usually guided by his own associations of ideas with the word, the connotations which it chiefly has for him—or sometimes, in the case of those for whom 'Romantic' is an adjective of disparagement, guided only by a determination to apply that damning epithet to all the ideas or tastes which they most dislike. The result of this sort of procedure is not only the vast terminological confusion to which I have already referred, but a vast amount of bad history—the reading into texts or doctrines which have come to be commonly classified as 'Romantic,' of all characteristics or theses which one has, by a largely *a priori,* non-historical method, determined to be the pure quiddity of 'the Romantic,' *das Wesen des Romantischen.* These are, I am aware, dogmatic-sounding assertions; but probative examples could be cited by the dozen. . . . Nothing, then, but confusion and error can result from the quest of some suppositious intrinsic nature of a hypostatized essence called 'Romanticism.'[4]

One highly important concept, especially in its relation to time, is that of organism, in the logical sense. This, however, would require so elaborate a historical analysis that I have reluctantly felt constrained to omit any such analysis in the present volume.

I wish to express my thanks to the American Council of Learned Societies for the very handsome grant which made the publication of this volume possible;

[4] "The Meaning of Romanticism for the Historian of Ideas," *Journal of the History of Ideas,* June, 1941, pp. 259-60.

and also my acknowledgements to the Harvard University Press for permitting me to quote in Lecture V certain passages from Chapter XI of *The Great Chain of Being.*

The greater part of the following lectures is a revision and expansion of a course given at Princeton University on the Spencer Trask Foundation in 1939. Though an excessively long time has elapsed between the original delivery of the lectures and their present expanded and revised form, it is improbable that they would even yet have been ready for publication at this time if I had not enjoyed the help of Mr. Bernard R. Mathews, Jr., an advanced graduate student in the department of philosophy at Johns Hopkins University, as research assistant. A considerable part of the final version, especially of Lecture V, is the result of discussions between him and the author on the issues involved.

Baltimore *A. O. Lovejoy*
*January 9, 1961*

# *Lecture I*

Characteristic of nearly all the more typical and influential of the philosophic systems which introduced a new temper into German and eventually into European thought between 1795 and 1830 was a fashion of distinguishing two radically different modes of knowing, a "lower" and a "higher," of which the former was said to constitute the method of science, the latter that of philosophy. This fashion appeared in several somewhat differing forms. But in all its forms it was marked by a depreciation of what was called "the ordinary logic" and also of sense-perception as means of becoming acquainted with "reality"—with the true nature of things; and its representatives all proclaimed that there is in man another cognitive "faculty," a different way of knowing, unrecognized by most earlier modern philosophy, through which he can gain a veritable and certain access to Being as it actually is. To some of the most eminent and influential minds of that period this reputed discovery in epistemology seemed the most important event of their age—far more momentous than

1

such transient and external episodes as the French Revolution or the rise and fall of the Napoleonic Empire.

There were some earlier eighteenth-century fore-shadowings of this new doctrine—for example, in that queer prophetic figure, Johann Georg Hamann. But it was Friedrich Heinrich Jacobi who gave it its most powerful impetus and provided the most familiar ter-minology for its principal thesis, in the celebrated antithesis of "the Understanding" and "the Reason." The distinction between these two so-called "facul-ties," *Verstand* and *Vernunft,* had, indeed, been made, and much insisted upon, by Kant; but he seemed to Jacobi to have reversed the proper relations of the two. The former term in the Kantian vocabulary repre-sented those relational forms which, in perception and thought, the mind, out of its own resources, imposes—as he believed—upon what would otherwise be an unrelated and meaningless chaos of sensations. The "concepts of the Understanding," though not derived from sense-experience, had for Kant pertinency or validity only when their application is limited to sense-experience; since they tell us what such experi-ence *must* be *for us,* they enable us to discover uni-versal laws to which it can be known in advance that all sensibly experienced phenomena will conform; but this is their sole function. The only legitimate use of these concepts and laws, in short, is what Kant calls their "immanent" use; our minds, however, tend to give them a "transcendent" application, to suppose that they are sources of information about things-in-themselves, or about the totality of experience, not merely about the manner in which particular concrete bits of subjective experience will always be related one to another. When their application is illegitimately extended, when they are taken as affording answers to the larger questions which our minds inevitably ask, these Ideas mislead us; they take our thought beyond its depth. This was not, in fact, precisely Kant's final position, but Jacobi supposed it to be; and it was to this apparently negative outcome of the Kantian theoretical philosophy that he fundamentally objected. While Kant had, Jacobi wrote in 1801 (in the preface of his essay *On the Attempt of the Critical Philosophy to Subject the Reason to the Understanding*), nominally represented "the Reason as sitting in the Upper House, the Understanding in the Lower," he had ascribed all real rights of cognition to the latter alone, as "the representative of the faculty of Sensibility, which is the true Sovereign, without whose ratification nothing has validity." "The Kantian theory," Jacobi continued, "has for its aim to warn the Understanding against the Reason as a deceiver, and thus to safeguard it against the

Reason's seductions." To Jacobi, on the other hand, it was the peculiarly limited mode of knowing which Kant called "the Understanding" that was the real enemy of all genuine philosophy, at least so far as it asserted its pretensions at the expense of its rightful overlord, the Reason.

What Jacobi was here expressing in figurative language was the thesis that we have a power, however seldom exercised, not merely to imagine, postulate or believe in, but to *know*, with the most indubitable kind of knowledge, a realm of realities other than that of sense-experience, and not subject to the categories and laws which hold good of the sensible world. This knowledge is not the result of any process of inference, it is not mediated through general concepts; it is a direct "intuiting" or "perceiving" of "the supersensible," analogous, in its immediacy and indubitability, to physical vision, though differing from it utterly in the nature of that which it discloses. This power, then—for the present only incompletely and vaguely defined—is the "Reason" of which Jacobi proclaimed the supremacy.

In Jacobi, as the originator of this fashion of glorifying something usually called "the Reason" at the expense of "the Understanding," what a later writer has called "the new problem of Romanticism," came to consciousness, that of "rediscovering the source, the root, of all ideas and all problems, the 'blue flower' of knowledge."[1] The effect upon the minds of Jacobi's contemporaries was the sort of effect which the same type of doctrine, when it is new or seems new, may always be expected to produce, if promulgated with ardor and with rhetorical impressiveness. The human spirit seemed by this discovery—not simply of a new piece of philosophical argument, but of an unsuspected power of direct insight—to be suddenly released from its accustomed limitations; philosophy seemed new-equipped with wings; and those to whom the revelation came often began to speak in rather strange tongues, as, for example, the young Friedrich Schlegel, in the letters which he wrote to his brother in the early seventeen-nineties on *"Jacobi's Vernunft."*[2]

The importance of the rôle of Jacobi as the initiator of new tendencies in German philosophy is even yet, as a rule, too little appreciated; as a historic influence he is hardly second to Kant. "It will scarcely be denied," wrote Hegel in 1817, in his estimate of Jacobi's historical significance, "that it has been the joint work of Jacobi and Kant to have put an end to the sort of metaphysics which had up to that time

[1] F. A. Schmid, *Friedrich Heinrich Jacobi* (1908), p. 300.
[2] Cf. Walzel's *Friedrich Schlegel's Briefe* (Berlin, 1890), pp. 49, 124, 126, 142.

prevailed—to have put an end not so much to its content as to its methodology of knowledge—and to have established the necessity for a completely altered conception of the logical. Jacobi has thus made a definitive epoch in the history of German philosophy, and, since philosophy outside of Germany has become entirely extinct, in the history of philosophy in general."[3] The whole generation of German thinkers whose philosophical ideas began to take form between 1785-95 were powerfully affected by Jacobi's writings. Fichte, for example, in 1794 sent Jacobi, whom he had never met, advance sheets of his *Grundlagen der Wissenschaftslehre*, and declared: "If there is any thinker in Germany with whom I should especially wish and hope to be in agreement, it is yourself." The older philosopher seemed to the younger "the noblest figure of pure humanity which our age can show." In 1795 Fichte wrote: "I have this summer been reading your writings again and again and yet again, and I am astonished, especially in *Allwill*,[4] by

[3] From Hegel's review of the third volume of Jacobi's *Werke*, in Hegel's *Werke* (1835), XVII, 30. Some of Hegel's earlier comments on Jacobi, written in a more controversial temper, were less appreciative.

[4] Jacobi's novel in epistolary form, *Allwills Briefsammlung* (1774). The citations are from *Fichte's Leben und literarischer Briefwechsel*, vol. II, edited by his son.

the striking similarity of our philosophical views. The public will hardly believe that this similarity exists; possibly you yourself will not do so." The similarity, in truth, fell considerably short of identity, and Jacobi was destined before his death to engage in vigorous and in some cases embittered, controversies with most of the younger leaders in the new speculative movement—with Fichte himself, with Schelling, Friedrich Schlegel, and Hegel. As often happens with initiators of revolutions, the forces which he had put into action soon passed beyond his control; the ideas which he had planted in younger men's minds developed into forms upon which he was able to look with small satisfaction. It remains none the less true that certain of the most pregnant of the new conceptions had been first cultivated by him; and that, in particular, the characteristic peculiarities of the new intuitionist theory of knowledge owed more to his teaching than to Kant's.

Nevertheless, Kant had a share in the responsibility; he was the other grandfather of the theory. Grandfathers of the same child are not necessarily fond of one another; and in this case, each at times expressed his opinion of the other's philosophic character with considerable candor. To Kant, Jacobi's assertion of a possible direct perception of ultimate truth, not gained through arduous and sustained efforts of the laboring intellect, seemed the very negation of philosophy. He therefore viewed the growing influence of Jacobi upon the younger generation with alarm, and was finally moved to combat it. The immediate occasion of his onslaught was a disquisition on the method of philosophy and the sources of metaphysical knowledge appended to an edition of the Platonic Epistles by J. G. Schlosser, the brother-in-law of Goethe and a friend and ardent admirer of Jacobi. The attack took the form of an article in the *Berliner Monatsschrift* of May, 1796, entitled "On a Certain Genteel Tone which has of late appeared in Philosophy" (*Von einem neuerdings erhobenen vornehmen Ton in der Philosophie*). The article, if it contains less connected philosophical argument than is usual in Kant's writings, has a vivacity and humor which is rare in them; it is the liveliest thing he ever wrote. He evidently felt that the new fashion in epistemology neither deserved nor was likely to be affected by any serious and elaborate refutation, and he therefore relied chiefly upon the weapon of irony. Why "the philosophy of intuition" was described by him, in the title of the essay, as an attempt to introduce a more "genteel tone" into philosophy, is apparent from the following:

It is a consequence not only of the natural laziness but also of the vanity of men, that those who live

on the income from property which they own—be
it small or large—consider themselves more genteel
than those who have to work for their living. . . .
This tendency of human nature has of late reached
such a pitch that a so-called philosophy is now
advertised in which, in order to possess all philosophical wisdom, one has no need to work, but has
only to listen to and enjoy the oracle that speaks
within oneself. It is announced that those who follow
this philosophy . . . are able by a single penetrating
glance into their own inwards (*auf ihr Inneres*) to
accomplish all that others can achieve by the ut-
most industry—and, indeed, much more. In the
case of sciences which require work on the part of
those who study them—such as mathematics, the
natural sciences, ancient history, linguistics, and
philosophy itself, in so far as it is under the necessity of carrying out a methodical development and
systematic combination of concepts—many men, no
doubt, have manifested a certain pedantic *pride;*
but it is only the philosopher of intuition who can
assume this *genteel* air, since he alone discovers
his own nature, not by the herculean labor of self-
knowledge built up patiently from the foundations,
but by a sort of self-apotheosis which enables him
to soar above all this vulgar task-work. When he
speaks, it is upon his own authority; and there is
no one who is entitled to call him to account.

In a later passage the reference to Jacobi is still
more direct and unmistakable:

The pretension to philosophize under the influence of a higher *feeling* is best of all adapted to produce this genteel tone. For who will deny that I *have* the feeling? And if I can make people believe that this feeling is not merely a subjective peculiarity of my own, but can be possessed by everybody, and that consequently it is something objective, a genuine piece of knowledge attained, not by reasoning from concepts, but by an intuition which grasps the object itself—then I enjoy a great advantage over all those who must first justify their statements before they are entitled to regard them as true. . . . So hurrah for the philosophy of feeling, which leads us directly to the reality itself (*zur Sache selbst*)! Down with ratiocination by means of concepts, which seeks truth only through the round-about way of general notions, and before it gets any content which it can immediately grasp, demands determinate forms under which it may subsume that content! . . . There have hitherto been recognized [continues Kant in a more serious vein] only three degrees in the affirmation of the truth of a proposition: the proposition may be known to be true, it may be probable, or it may be a matter of opinion (*meinen*). But there is now introduced a new kind of cognition which has nothing in common with logic and involves no process of the Understanding but is a sort of anticipatory sensing (*praevisio sensitiva*) of something that is not an object of sense; which in other words, is a *presentiment* (*Ahnung*) of the supersensible.[5]

---

[5] *Ahnung* was one of Jacobi's names for his "intuition."

The real purpose, Kant declares, of those who preach this doctrine is, "under the name of philosophy, to make an end of philosophy altogether; they are not philosophers but mystery-mongers (*Geheimniskrämer*)." Doubtless the ultimate end at which they aim is praiseworthy enough; "the veiled goddess before whom they too bow the knee is none other than the moral law within us in its inviolable majesty." And it may perhaps be conceded "that after the moral law has been formulated and vindicated by genuinely philosophical methods, it is permissible to lend additional vividness to the idea of it by those essentially aesthetic and analogical modes of expression which writers of this school are fond of employing." But there is always the danger that these mere fashions of speech will be taken literally and that people will be led thereby to fall "into those enthusiastic and visionary modes of thought (*in schwärmerische Visionen*) which are the death of all philosophy." The truth is, Kant concludes, that "philosophy is fundamentally prosaic; and to attempt to philosophize poetically is very much as if a merchant should undertake to make up his account-books not in prose but in verse."

In spite of these exchanges of compliments between the two philosophers, their doctrines—or the implications of their doctrines—were less radically different and irreconcilable than both at times supposed. Certainly it was far from exact to say, as Jacobi said, that Kant had unequivocally ascribed a superior cognitive role to the Understanding. For the first *Kritik* had left that "faculty"—in other words, the notions of space and time, the categories, the laws of sense-experience, including that of causality—it had left these completely discredited, as means of knowing either what "things" are in themselves or what we are in ourselves. The Understanding presents merely a world of appearances, of which the constitutive pattern is the creation of our minds. It is a function that betrays its deficiencies by involving us in hopeless contradictions, or leading us up blind alleys, as soon as we attempt to think through, or to apply comprehensively, the concepts by which it operates. The term "the *Pure* Reason" was only another name for "the Understanding," when the Understanding is taken seriously as an organ of metaphysical knowledge; and the negative result of the *Kritik* was, notoriously, a proof that the "Pure" Reason is *not* an organ of such knowledge. *If* anything more than the general forms and rules of the interconnection of particular sensible phenomena is to be known, it is not the concepts of the Understanding that can disclose it to us, it is not in the Understanding's world of space and time and causality, and the rest, that it is to be looked for. True, if Kant had stopped here, the conclusion to be drawn would have been that nothing more *is* to be looked for, that metaphysics is impossible; and Kant might have seemed to be what Mendelssohn called him—*der Alleszermalmende*. But Kant did not stop here. For his so-called "Practical Reason," which had the last word in his philosophy, gave forth metaphysical as well as ethical deliverances; and though the former were called "Postulates," and were sometimes described by him as propositions to be accepted by faith on the ground of their needfulness as a support for morals, to one of them he assigned no such equivocal status; *it,* he declared, is "a matter of fact" (*Thatsache*) not a "matter of faith" (*Glaubenssache*)—a fact of which "the objective reality can be shown through experience."[6] And *what* Kant thus in the end proclaimed with complete assurance was the reality of a supersensible realm of being, to which *we* belong—an "intelligible" or "noumenal" world,

[6] See *Kr. d. Urteilskraft*, A,451. The potential objects of knowledge are here divided into three classes: *Sachen der Meinung* (*opinabilia*); *Thatsachen* (*scibilia*); *Glaubenssachen* (*credibilia*). Now, Kant observes, alone among the *Vernunftideen*, the "Idea of Freedom" is a *Thatsache;* for this, "as the 'Idea' of a special sort of causality, can be demonstrated through the practical laws of the Pure Reason and, in conformity with these, be manifested in actual deeds (*in wirklichen Handlungen*), and therefore, in experience." But this freedom is solely a property of the *Noumenal Ego;* therefore, the existence of this supratemporal Ego, "as *causa noumenon*," is not problematical merely, but positively demonstrable.

similar to Plato's, in so far as its inmates were declared to be wholly alien to time and space and the
goings-on of nature, but different from Plato's in that
they consist, not of hypostatized universals—Platonic
Ideas—but of eternalized individuals—noumenal
Egos, *i.e.*, Selves not in space nor in time nor en-
meshed in matter. Perhaps the most important thing to
bear in mind about the Kantian doctrine as a historical
influence in the period 1790–1830 is that it was—to
use the concise German labels—a *Zweiweltenlehre*
and even a *Zweiwahrheitenlehre*. Philosophy, Kant
also in the end held, reveals with certainty another
*kind* of world, unknown to sense and to science, dis-
coverable by a different method, more direct than
any labored concatenation of "concepts of the theoretical Understanding." It was chiefly by virtue of this
strain in it that the Critical Philosophy could, in de-
spite of its author, co-operate with the influence of
Jacobi in the production of that complex of ideas
which we are to examine;[7] and it was this aspect of

[7] Jacobi later recognized and emphasized this affinity between Kant's doctrine and his own: Speaking of "a higher
faculty, which gives knowledge of the True in and above
phenomena, in a manner incomprehensible to the senses and
the Understanding," Jacobi observes: "It is upon such a
higher faculty that the Kantian philosophy also is really based"
(Introduction to the 1815 edition of *David Hume über den
Glauben*).

it above all that won for "Transcendentalism" the
enthusiastic acceptance of those who were to give new
impulsions to British and American thought—Coleridge, Carlyle, Emerson. About much of Kant's system
—about the greater part (and the difficult part) of
the *Critique of Pure Reason*—they knew and cared
little, I fear; they were all of them somewhat "genteel," in the sense in which Kant had used the word;
they did not like to work very hard for their philosophical convictions, though they happily believed
this to be unnecessary because the hard work was
supposed to have already been done once for all by
Kant. And the Kant whose teaching they accepted as
conclusive was not the author of the satire on Jacobi's
"philosophy of intuition"; it was a Kant whose chief
reputed discovery, though reached by a different road,
was almost identical with Jacobi's. "The grand characteristic of Kant's philosophy," wrote Carlyle in the
*Edinburgh Review* in 1827, is the "distinction . . .
between Understanding and Reason," and what he
supposed this to imply is made evident in the highly
rhetorical passage that follows:

> The Kantists . . . [said Carlyle] believe that both
> Understanding and Reason are organs, or rather,
> we should say, modes of operation, by which the
> mind discovers truth; but they think that their man-
> ner of proceeding is essentially different; that their

provinces are separate and distinguishable, nay, that it is of the first importance to separate and distinguish them. Reason, the Kantists say, is of a higher nature than the Understanding; it works by more subtle methods, on higher objects, and requires a far finer culture for its development, indeed, in many men it is never developed at all; but its results are no less certain, nay, they are much more so; for Reason discerns Truth itself, the absolutely and primitively *True;* while Understanding discerns only relations, and cannot decide without an if. . . . Not by logic and argument does it [Reason] work; yet surely and clearly may it be taught to work; and its domain lies in that higher region whither logic and argument cannot reach; in that holier region where Poetry and Virtue and Divinity abide, in whose presence Understanding wavers and recoils, dazzled into utter darkness by that "sea of light," at once the fountain and the termination of true knowledge.[8]

The temper and rhetorical tone here are Jacobian (and Schellingian) and not Kantian, and so, in part, are the ideas—so far as there can be said to be ideas. What Carlyle said "the Kantists say" was precisely what Jacobi had once said that Kant himself denied. Nevertheless, there was, as we have seen, an element

[8] *The State of German Literature,* pp. 348–49. See also Carlyle's passage on the subject in his essay on Novalis, 1829, where he himself intimates that his exposition of the distinction is possibly more Jacobian than Kantian.

in Kant's own doctrine which was not altogether incongruous with this attempt of Carlyle's to elucidate
the great distinction to the British mind.

Coleridge, it will be remembered, made his theological apologetic in *Aids to Reflection* turn almost
entirely upon a proof that man possesses the faculty
of Reason and that it "differs in kind" from the Understanding. He tells his readers that "the main chance
of their *reflecting* on religious subjects *aright*, and of
their attaining to the *contemplation* of spiritual truths
*at all*, depends on their insight into the *nature* of this
disparity" between Understanding and Reason, and
"on their conviction of its existence." For Reason
alone "is the Source and Substance of Truths above
Sense and having their evidence in themselves," and
thus our only means of access to the supersensible
world with which religion is concerned.[9]

Emerson, too, felt the need of translating some of
the familiar antitheses of the Christian dualism into
the new and, as he conceived, more "scientific" terminology. He wrote in his *Journal* in 1833: "Jesus
Christ was a minister of Pure Reason. The beatitudes
of the Sermon on the Mount are all utterances of the
mind contemning the phenomenal world. . . . The

[9] *Aids to Reflection:* "Aphorisms on Spiritual Religion,"
VIII. Coleridge's conception of the distinction has peculiarities
of its own which will be noted in a subsequent lecture.

Understanding can make nothing of it. 'Tis all non-
sense. The Reason affirms its absolute verity. Various
terms are employed to indicate the counteraction of
the Reason and the Understanding, with more or less
precision, according to the cultivation of the speaker.
A clear perception of it is the key to all theology, and
a theory of human life. When Novalis says 'It is the
instinct of the Understanding to counteract the Reason,' he only translates into a scientific formula the
sentence of St. Paul, 'The carnal mind is enmity
against God.' "[10] A year later Emerson writes at length
on the subject to his brother Edward:

> Philosophy affirms that the outward world is only
> phenomenal & the whole concern of dinners of
> tailors of gigs of balls whereof men make such ac-
> count is a quite relative and temporary one—an
> intricate dream—the exhalation of the present state
> of the Soul—wherein the Understanding works in-
> cessantly as if it were real but the eternal Reason
> when now & then he is allowed to speak declares
> it is an accident a smoke nowise related to his
> permanent attributes. Now that I have used the
> words, let me ask do you draw the distinction of
> Milton Coleridge & the Germans between Reason &

[10] Vol. III, pp. 236–37; Perry's *The Heart of Emerson's
Journals*, p. 81. The same application of the Pauline phrase to
the Understanding was made by Coleridge: "Notes on Leigh-
tion," in *Literary Remains* (*Works*, ed. Shedd, V, 378). But
Emerson presumably could not have seen this in 1833.

Understanding. I think it a philosophy itself & like all truth very practical. So now lay aside the letter & take up the following dissertation on Sunday.

The "dissertation" runs thus:

Reason is the highest faculty of the soul—what we mean often by the soul itself; it never *reasons*, never proves, it simply perceives; it is vision. The Understanding toils all the time, compares, contrives, adds, argues, near-sighted but strong-sighted, dwelling in the present the expedient the customary. Beasts have some Understanding but no Reason. Reason is potentially perfect in every man—Understanding in very different degrees of strength. The thoughts of youth, & "first thoughts," are the revelations of Reason, the love of the beautiful & of Goodness as the highest beauty the belief in the absolute & universal superiority of the Right & the True. But Understanding that wrinkled calculator the steward of our house to whom is committed the support of our animal life contradicts evermore the affirmations of Reason & points at Custom & Interest & persuades one man that the declarations of Reason are false and another that they are at least impracticable. . . . The manifold applications of the distinction to Literature to the Church to Life will show how good a key it is. So hallelujah to Reason for evermore.[11]

But the terminology by which Jacobi, and sometimes Kant, had expressed the contrast between the

[11] *Letters* (1939), I, 412–13.

two modes of knowledge—and which, through its use by Carlyle and Coleridge, has become the most familiar one in English—was not that most commonly employed by the German philosophers who shared Jacobi's conviction of the superiority of the Reason to the Understanding as the origin of philosophical knowledge. The word "Reason" alone did not sufficiently indicate the nature of that superior kind of apprehension to which the Understanding is unable to rise. In common usage the two terms have almost the same meaning; and "Reason" does not naturally suggest the peculiarity of the true philosophical insight —the peculiarity upon which Jacobi himself had insisted; namely, its directness or immediacy. For the antithetic to "Understanding," therefore, Fichte and Schelling adopted the term "intellectual intuition" (*intellektuelle Anschauung*) (or, if you prefer that translation, "intellectual perception"), or sometimes "intuition of Reason."[12] The term has a long prior

[12] Cf. Schelling's *Philosophische Briefe über Dogmatismus und Kritizismus* (1795). The term Vernunft-Anschauung was later adopted by Jacobi also (*Werke*, II, 59–60): "This, above all else, is to be firmly held: that as there is a sensuous intuition, so there is also a rational intuition, an intuition through the Reason. The two stand as distinctive sources of knowledge over against one another; . . . and similarly, both stand in the same relation to the Understanding, and, in so far, also to demonstration. . . . We must use the term 'intuition of Reason'

history, but to go into it is not to the present purpose. It too was an expression to which Kant had recently helped to give currency. In several passages he contrasts "sensible intuition," familiar to us in our perceptual experience, with a possible "intellectual intuition" such as natural theology had ascribed to the deity, the *Urwesen*. The latter mode of perception is distinguished, not only by its assumed freedom from the forms of time and space and the categories of the Understanding, but above all by the assumption that its object is not given to it from without; *i.e.*, the object and the subject in it are not mutually external. But the possibility for us mortals of such a direct quasi-perceptual knowledge Kant had (though inconsistently) denied.[13] Fichte had, however, used the term to express the Ego's immediate consciousness

---

*(Vernunft-Anschauung)*, because language possesses no other to indicate the manner and mode in which that which is unattainable by the senses is given to the Understanding in overflowing *(überschwenglich)* feelings alone, and yet as something truly objective, which it has by no means merely invented *(erdachte)*."

[13] The term as used by Kant was derived from the Neoplatonic, Patristic, and Scholastic tradition; for a brief indication of the earlier usage, cf. Eisler, *Wörterbuch der philosophischen Begriffe, s.v.* "Anschauung, intellektuale." The passages in Kant in which the term or idea occurs are *De mundo sensibili,* II, no. 10; *Kr. d. r. V.,* A, 256; *Kr. d. pr. V.,* A, 178, 247–48; *Prolegg.,* 107, 172.

of its own activity: the immediate consciousness that I am doing something and what I am doing; this is that by which I know something because I am doing it (*das unmittelbare Bewusstsein, dass ich handle und was ich handle; sie ist das, wodurch ich etwas weiss, weil ich es tue*). Neither the term nor the notion, then, was of Schelling's invention; and there is a measure of justification for the elegantly expressed remark of Liebmann that the *intellektuelle Anschauung* was simply "raked out of Kant's soiled linen."[14] But it was Schelling who, among his contemporaries, employed the term most copiously, and, on the whole, did most to develop the ideas connected with it, while (though at a later date) he violently repudiated Jacobi's way of expressing the antithesis, on various grounds—among them, that "in all languages until the Kantian confusion of tongues, the term 'Understanding' has always been the name given to the higher faculty." This, however, was largely a matter of taste in nomenclature, and Schelling's vehemence with regard to it was probably due to the fact that, being then engaged in a violent attack upon the older man, he was simply hitting at every feature of Jacobi's philosophy of which he caught sight.

Among the early nineteenth-century followers of Kant, the chief protestant against this terminology was

[14] *Kant und die Epigonen* (1865), p. 94.

Schopenhauer; but it is, in reality, solely against the language of his contemporaries, and not against the essential ideas expressed by it, that he protests. He has the air, indeed, of condemning roundly the entire pretension of Jacobi and Schelling and their disciples to the possession of a higher faculty of "Reason."

The truth is [he declares], they wanted Reason's place and name for a faculty of their own devising, or, to speak more accurately, for a completely fictitious faculty, designed to help them out of the straits in which Kant had left them; a faculty for direct metaphysical knowledge: that is to say, one which transcends all possible experience, is able to grasp the world of things-in-themselves and their relations, and is therefore, before all, a consciousness of God. . . . During the last half-century, however, there has been a considerable divergence of opinion among adepts as to the way in which all these supersensible glories are to be perceived. According to the most audacious [Schelling], Reason has an immediate intuition, or vision, of the Absolute, or even *ad libitum* of the Infinite and its evolution into the finite. . . . The most modest of these adepts declare that the "Reason" has neither a "vision" nor an "audition" of these glories, but a mere *Ahndung*, or vague misgiving of them.[15]

[15] *Fourfold Root of the Principle of Sufficient Reason*, 2d edition, 34 (Eng. tr., Bohn Lib., pp. 131 ff.).

Of these audacities Schopenhauer, when engaged in cudgelling his elder contemporaries, professes himself incapable:

> *My* philosophy does not for a moment accept the fable—so cleverly devised by the professors of philosophy, and now become indispensable to them —of a Reason possessing an absolute and immediate knowledge or intuition or "audition," which they are accustomed to fasten upon their readers at the outset, and thereupon to draw them without difficulty, as by a four-horse team, into that region beyond all possible experience which Kant wholly and forever barred to human knowledge.[16]

This appearance of contrast between his own epistemological procedure and Schelling's Schopenhauer gains partly by misrepresenting his rival's real meaning, chiefly by glossing over, for the occasion, certain of the most fundamental and distinctive of his own philosophical principles. Behind the diversity of phraseology, as our later examination of both systems will readily show, lies a large measure of identity in substance of doctrine.

So much for the immediate antecedents of the general doctrine, the variant terminology in which it was expressed, and some examples of the enthusiastic

[16] Preface to Second Edition (1844) of *The World as Will and Idea* (Eng. tr., Haldane and Kemp, London, 1883, p. XXIX).

utterances about it of those who accepted it as a
new philosophic revelation. But from the utterances
thus far cited no one can have gained any very clear
notion of what the revelation revealed. What it was
supposed to reveal, and how, we must attempt to see
by a closer and more analytical observation of this
historical phenomenon—a resolution of it into the
rather numerous, and sometimes mutually incongruous, ideas and philosophic motives which composed it or explained its vogue. The exposition of
these will in most cases take its starting point in passages in the early writings of Schelling concerning
the "intellectual intuition," but its purpose is less to
summarize the teachings (on this subject) of an individual philosopher than to distinguish (and at the
same time to correlate) a number of ideas current in
Germany through the two opening decades of the nineteenth century, and in most cases also widely influential and diversely affecting thinkers in other countries
and at later periods who were directly or indirectly
influenced by these German writers. Schelling was
merely the most systematic and most complete elab-
orator of thoughts which came to him and to his generation largely from the older contemporaries mentioned—and from some still older sources. Some of
the ideas which we are to scrutinize were not peculiar
to this group but were also shared by numerous other

writers. There is a saying of Goethe's which, though exaggerated, has much truth in it: "that which is in the air, and which the age demands, may spring up in a hundred minds at once, without any borrowing by one from another." The series of interconnected (which does not always mean mutually consistent) ideas which we are to review, was very diffusely in the air as the eighteenth century was ending and the nineteenth beginning.

But it was not of that age alone that this is true. Many of the same ideas appear to have been "demanded" over again almost precisely a century later, initially but by no means solely in France. Henri Bergson performed in his earlier writings, for his generation, approximately the rôle that some of the German philosophers had performed for theirs; the most characteristic parts of his philosophy closely reproduce most of the typical elements of the theory of knowledge of Schelling and his school.[17] How far the

[17] That Bergson's anti-intellectualism has a close kinship with what is commonly called the spirit of Romanticism in philosophy has already been remarked by several writers, *e.g.* by Professor Frank Thilly in his presidential address before the American Philosophical Association, 1912 (published in the *Philosophical Review*, 1913, pp. 107–32). But the specifications in justifications of the analogy have not, I believe, hitherto been fully presented, though a number of them have been pointed out by G. Jäger, *Das Verhältnis Bergson's zu Schelling* (1917); E.

parallelism is due to a direct or indirect influence of the German writers in question upon the thought of the most celebrated and influential of recent French philosophers, it is not especially important to inquire. It is conceivable that the same conceptions again germinated independently in another mind, though it seems more probable that their reappearance was due to the continuous preservation of the seeds of them—especially of certain elements of the Schellingian tradition—in French philosophy of the mid-nineteenth century. However that may be, I think it may be of interest to present the parallelism where it occurs, point by point, in order to make evident the fact that the same theory of knowledge has been one of the factors in the movement of ideas in our own century.

Before proceeding to the connected presentation of the more specific conceptions which make up this theory of knowledge, it is well to guard against a possible misconception of its general implications. It is somewhat misleading to speak of this scheme of ideas without qualification as a species of anti-intellectualism. In some of the uses made of it, especially when it became popularized and was given application in various fields by men of letters and other non-

Bréhier, *Schelling* (1912) ; C. Dyrssen, *Bergson und die deutsche Romantik* (1912) ; J. R. Richter, *"Intuition" und "intellektuelle Anschauung" bei Schelling und Bergson* (1929).

philosophers, it sometimes did make for obscurantism and for a distrust of scientific methods as such. But though it became the fashion to speak condescendingly, and even contemptuously, of the unfortunate *Verstand*, which admittedly was the "organ" of scientific inquiry, this was not usually meant to imply that the Understanding is not all very well in its place. It has the respectability which attaches to usefulness; indeed, with respect to it, a theory having some kinship with pragmatism—or with one of the pragmatisms—was a commonplace for the epistemologists who held this view. The operation of the *Verstand* and the limits of its validity are to be understood solely in the light of its practical utility. It does not make us acquainted with the nature of things or of ourselves, but only with the conditions of effectiveness in the practical and physical business of everyday life; its truth is a purely pragmatic truth. Thus Jacobi writes:

> If, by "Reason," we mean man's soul only in so far as it possesses clear concepts—only in so far as it is Understanding—. . . then Reason is merely a piece of property belonging to a man, a tool (*Werkzeug*) of which he makes use. If, however, we mean by Reason the principle of knowledge as such, then it is the spirit of which the whole living nature of

man is constituted; it is to it that man belongs; he is a form which it has assumed.[18]

So Carlyle, in one of his attempts to elucidate the distinction:

The proper province of Understanding is all, strictly speaking, real, practical and material knowledge: mathematics, physics, political economy, the adaptation of means to ends in the whole business of life. In this province, it is the strength and universal implement of the mind; an indispensable servant without which, indeed, existence itself would be impossible. Let it not step beyond this province, however, not usurp the province of Reason, which it is appointed to obey, and cannot rule over without ruin to the whole spiritual man.[19]

Schopenhauer caught up and made much of this tool-theory of the intellect. Knowledge was originally destined for the service of the will. The "intellect" exists exclusively for practical ends. It is "by no means designed for deciphering the inner nature of things and of the world." Yet, of course, Schopenhauer holds that by some other mode of apprehension than "intellect" that nature *may* be deciphered. Even the biological or Darwinian way of phrasing this doc-

[18] Jacobi *Werke*, Bd. IV. *Beilagen zu den Briefen über die Lehre des Spinoza* (1819), p. 153.

[19] *Ibid.*, p. 348. Cf. also the conclusion of the passage from Goethe's *Conversations with Eckermann*, cited below.

trine of the exclusively practical rôle of this faculty may be found anticipated in Schopenhauer; for him too the intellect is simply an instrument of adaptation to environment and an aid to survival in the struggle for existence. He quotes with approval a remark of Cuvier's: "The conservation of species depends not less upon the intellectual than the physical qualities of animals," and adds: "This confirms my principle that the intellect, like the claws and teeth, is nothing else than a weapon in the service of the will."[20] The knowing function "far from being absolutely first (as, for example, Fichte teaches) is at bottom tertiary, for it presupposes the [bodily] organism, and the organism presupposes the will."[21] The "progress in the development of the brain, and thus of the intellect," corresponds to the "ascending scale of animal organization," and is, like all the other forward steps of Nature, brought about by the constantly increasing and more complicated *needs* of the series of organisms —since Nature provides "every animal with the organs which are necessary for its sustenance and the weapons necessary for the conflict that it must wage." Man is of all animals the most highly endowed with intelligence because, on the one hand, his more complex organization makes his wants more numerous,

[20] *World as Will and Idea* (Eng. tr.), II, 166.
[21] *Ibid.*, p. 13.

and because, on the other hand, he is one of the most ill-provided among animals in his physical equipment for the struggle with his rivals. In him, however, the development of the intellect has gone so far that he is capable, in philosophy and in art, of "separating willing from knowing," of employing the intellect for other than practical ends.

This part of Schopenhauer's doctrine was accurately summarized by his faithful disciple and earliest commentator, Frauenstädt:

Schopenhauer discovered what the intellect is, in its origin and function, and to what class of phenomena it belongs: namely, that it is nothing but a tool, an organ of the will, a means to the preservation of the individual and the species; that, therefore, so far from being anything primary, fundamental, the heart and essence of all things, it, on the contrary, makes its first appearance in Nature only when some being is, through its possession of more developed, complicated and specific needs, compelled to extend the sphere of its existence beyond the limits of its own body. Through this deduction of the intellect, Schopenhauer not only came to the Kantian result, that the intellect is limited to mere phenomena; he also showed the true and ultimate reason *why* it *must* be limited to mere phenomena.[22]

[22] *Briefe über die Schopenhauer'sche Philosophie* (Leipzig, 1854), pp. 161–62.

Here is precisely that pragmatic form of idealism which is the true essence—however often forgotten —of Bergson's doctrine, or at least of one phase of his doctrine, about the physical world. That world for him is "phenomenal" in the Kantian sense—namely, that "all that it has that is intelligible is our own work"—but not for the Kantian reason. The "Kantian criticism is definitive in what it denies"; but "in what it affirms" it does not "give us the solution of the problem." The solution is that the intellect produces the *a priori* "form" of space as an instrument for action. "Space is the plan of our possible action on things. It is a view taken by mind. It is an idea that symbolizes the tendency of the human intellect to fabrication." And the "faculty of fabricating artificial objects, in particular, tools for making other tools . . . appears to be the original activity of the intellect."[23]

A sort of biological pragmatism is, then, what the Germans call a *"moment"* in the theory of knowledge we are considering. But this instrumentalist account of the office and nature of the "intellect" is equivalent to a denial of the fitness of that faculty to serve as the organ of metaphysical insight. For it is a primary assumption of all epistemologists of this group—the grounds for which will become more fully apparent

[23] *Creative Evolution* (New York, 1911), pp. 157, 205.

in the sequel—that the knowledge which is useful, because concerned with sensible objects and with relations of cause and effect or means and ends, does not yield philosophical truths, since, as Schopenhauer put it, no such knowledge gives us any acquaintance with "the real nature of things."[24] The human mind, writes Bergson, when regarded as working for practical utility, "is the object which psychology, as a natural science, studies"; but "metaphysics is this same mind striving to transcend the conditions of useful action and come back to itself as pure creative energy."

---

[24] *World as Will and Idea* (Eng. tr.), III, 21.

# Lecture II

1. What I am now to attempt is a task which may appear impossible because self-contradictory—namely, to elucidate what is by hypothesis incapable of elucidation. For the first thing to be observed about the new theory of knowledge is that it is professedly a mystery, in the Greek sense of the word. The saving intuition is not to be reached by any process of intellection, but by a sudden revelation; and except a man be born again he cannot receive it. The habits of thought characteristic of the ordinary Understanding must be cast off. In Schelling's words:

> All misunderstanding of the transcendental philosophy is due, not to any unintelligibility in that philosophy, but to a lack of the organ by which it must be apprehended. . . . Unless a man already brings the transcendental way of thinking with him, the transcendental philosophy must always be found unintelligible. It is therefore necessary that one insert oneself into this manner of thinking at the outset, through an act of freedom.[1]

[1] *Sämmtliche Werke*, 1 Abt., III: *System des transcendentalen Idealismus* (1800), pp. 367–70.

Schelling declared it to be his purpose "sharply to cut off the road of approach to philosophy, and so to isolate it on all sides from common knowledge that not a footpath shall lead from the latter to the former."[2] Coleridge was but paraphrasing Schelling when he wrote in the *Biographia Literaria:*

> To an Esquimaux or New Zealander, our most popular philosophy would be wholly unintelligible; for the sense, the inward organ, is not yet born in him. So is there many a one among us, yes, and some who think themselves philosophers, too, to whom the philosophic organ is entirely wanting. To such men philosophy is a mere play of words and notions, like a theory of music to the deaf.[3]

This tone is equally characteristic of the philosophy of Bergson. In the words of an exposition formally approved by him, "in order to understand Bergson, it is not necessary to have any previous acquaintance with philosophy, indeed the less the reader knows of current metaphysical notions the easier it may perhaps be for him to adopt the mental attitude required for understanding Bergson. For Bergson says that the tradition of philosophy is all wrong and must be

[2] *SW*, 1 Abt., IV, p. 362: *Fernere Darstellungen, usw.* (1802).

[3] *Biographia Literaria*, ch. 12, p. 173; cf. also pp. 164–66. The passage cited is apparently derived from Schelling's *System des transcendentalen Idealismus, SW*, I, IV, 370.

broken with; according to his view philosophical knowledge can only be obtained by 'a reversal of the usual work of the intellect.' "[4] As Mr. Walter Lippmann once put it, in a sympathetic account of this philosophy, "in a sense you must become a Bergsonian before you can understand Bergson."

It would appear, then, that only those who have already achieved the requisite emancipation from the ordinary habits of the intellect and have been initiated into the mystery can understand the doctrine—an awkward situation for the would-be expositor and historian. And what is worse, it is impossible even for the initiated, we are told, to express in words the truth which has been disclosed to them. For the adherers of this epistemology have always insisted upon the ineffableness of what is revealed in self intuition. It is an immediate knowledge of oneself, and by oneself, and cannot be imparted to another. The favorite word of Jacobi, as Lévy-Bruhl has remarked,[5] is *unaussprechlich*. And Schelling in one of his early writings declares that

> not even the language of Plato or of his spiritual kinsman Jacobi, can suffice to convey the distinction between absolute, immutable Being and conditioned, changeable existence. . . . This Absolute

[4] Karen Stephen, *The Misuse of Mind* (1922), p. 15.
[5] *La Philosophie de Jacobi* (1894), p. 63.

within us cannot, I think, be framed in human speech; only an intellectual intuition which one has gained for oneself (*selbsterrungenes Anschauen des Intellectualen*) can supplement the inadequacy of our language.[6]

Schopenhauer was reluctant to admit that his own system was a philosophy of the ineffable, since he was well aware of the humor there is in a philosopher's devoting many portly volumes to setting forth that which he at the same time declares to be unutterable in words. Yet there is no consequence which flows more obviously from Schopenhauer's primary principles, in the early version of his system, than the proposition that the true nature of things can never be expressed in "matter-moulded forms of speech." For that which is alien to the very constitutive forms of perception and thought manifestly must be beyond the reach of language, which is but the instrument of the Understanding—*i.e.*, of abstract thought, which is itself at two removes from reality. Schopenhauer, indeed, on occasion admits that it is only in the experiences of mystical ecstasy—experiences which are forever incapable of being *told*—that the *positive* meaning of the metaphysics of the Absolute Will can be apprehended; the discourse of the philosopher is rather devoted to telling what the Will is not. "Only

[6] *Vom Ich, usw.*; *SW*, 1 Abt., I, p. 216.

the worst knowledge, abstract, secondary knowledge, the concept, the mere shadow of true knowledge, is unconditionally communicable." For the conveyance of philosophical insight language is inadequate:

> To our own serious meditation and inward observation of things, speaking to others stands related as a machine to a living organism. . . . A man understands wholly only himself; others but half; for at best we can communicate only concepts, not the intuitional apprehension which lies behind the concepts. Consequently, deep philosophical truths can never be brought to light, after the common fashion of thought, by means of conversation. This last is, indeed, useful enough for intellectual exercise, for starting up problems, for ventilating them and afterwards for testing, checking-up and criticising the proposed solution. . . . But neither our knowledge nor our insight are ever much increased by discussing what has been said by others and coming to an agreement with them.[7]

Bergsonism, too, frankly belongs among the philosophies of the ineffable. At the end of a volume devoted to expounding the peculiarities of the "inner life," we are told that these "cannot be expressed in the fixed terms of language";[8] in fact, Bergson else-

[7] *Parerga and Paralipomena* (Eng. tr., Bohn Lib.), II, ch. 1, sec. 6, 7, pp. 166–67. Nothing more false, in my opinion, has ever been said about philosophy.

[8] *Time and Free Will*, (Eng. tr., London, 1910), p. 237.

where says, the philosophical intuition "is repugnant to the very essence of language." It may at first sight appear an embarrasing circumstance for a philosopher to have a message to convey which is, by his own confession, incapable of being put into words. But in point of fact, as the history of both philosophy and religion shows, there are few things which render a doctrine more attractive to many minds than an air of ineffability. Certainly the writings of most of Bergson's disciples show how greatly they have felt the fascination of this quality of mystical unutterableness in his doctrine. The adepts of this philosophy have often the air of going about with monitory fingers on lips and an expression of wondering rapture. One of Bergson's English translators has aptly prefixed to his version, with the author's permission, a motto from Plotinus which is in the true vein of Neoplatonic mysticism: "If a man were to inquire of Nature the reason of her creative activity and she were willing to give ear and answer, she would say—'Ask me not, but understand in silence, even as I am silent and am not wont to speak.' " "It is the idea of mystery," Georges Sorel said, "which should control the interpretation" of this (Bergson's) philosophy.

No subject, then, might seem less suitable for public discourse than such a theory of philosophical knowledge. But, happily for the lecturer, the philoso-

phers themselves, in spite of their commendation of a
wise silence, have provided him with abundant prec-
edent for public discourse about these matters; indeed, the philosophers of the ineffable have seldom
been the least loquacious of their kind. And the truth
is that the doctrine with which we are to be concerned
is by no means innocent of conceptual thought nor
insusceptible of analytical exposition. Of this the
proof must be found in the analysis which is to follow.
Meanwhile it must be borne in mind that the assumption that the nature of the "truly real" being is ineffable was not novel nor peculiar to the German philosophers who wrote so much about it. The positive
attributes of the God not only of Neoplatonism, but
of the medieval theology of Christendom—largely
derivative from Neoplatonism—and of the mystics of
all religions and all periods, had also been held to be
inexpressible in human language. Philosophy could
*tell* us only what God is *not;* the *via negativa,* the
denial of predicates alien to the essence of deity, was
the only strictly veridical way of speaking of the
Absolute Being.

       2. A more nearly differentiating
characteristic of this theory of knowledge is the direction in which it bids us look if we are to find and

grasp the true nature of reality. That direction is "inward"; "look in and not out" is the motto—the initial though not the final motto—of Schelling and most of the school. In short, the "intellectual intuition" is a *Selbstanschauung,* an intuition of oneself, or rather, of the innermost kernel of oneself; as a German writer on Schelling has observed, "between self-consciousness and *intellektuelle Anschauung* Schelling makes no distinction."[9] "We dream," said Novalis, "of travelling round the world; is the world not, then, within us? The depths of our own spirit we do not know. *Nach innen geht der geheimnisvolle Weg.*" The initiation into the mystery, then, consists in an introduction to our "real" or "deeper" selves.

> Only to one it was given to lift the veil of the goddess. What saw he then? He saw—wonder of wonders—himself!

Schleiermacher was equally insistent that the way of intuition meant looking inward rather than outward: "I can know another only through his deeds, for I never perceive his inner activity. . . . But a man's judgment cannot err when he turns his gaze only upon himself." "Whenever I turn my gaze back upon the

[9] J. R. Richter, *"Intuition" und "intellektuelle Anschauung" bei Schelling und Bergson* (1929), p. 18; the remark noted would be more precisely true if qualified by "primarily," as will later appear.

inner Self, I am forthwith in the realm of the eternal; I behold the activity of the Spirit, which the world cannot change, which time cannot destroy, but which, rather, creates both world and time."[10] Much of Schleiermacher's *Monologues* is simply a proclamation of the gospel of salvation through *Selbstbetrachtung*. Even the not altogether edifying hero of Friedrich Schlegel's *Lucinde* keeps in the fashion, by forming a resolution "to lose himself ever more deeply in the inner perspective of his own spirit."

Schopenhauer, too, assumed that, in contrast with the Understanding's knowledge of objects, which can never give us more than an acquaintance with mere phenomena, there is available to man an immediate knowledge of the very heart of reality as it is in itself, and that this knowledge must necessarily be self-knowledge. He formulates in the clearest terms the same methodology of philosophical insight, in its contrast with scientific knowledge:

> We, who have in view not etiology but philosophy, that is, not relative but unconditional knowledge of the real nature of the world, take the opposite course [to that of natural science], and start from that which is immediately and most completely known to us.[11]

[10] *Monologen* (1st ed., 1800), pp. 25, 31–32; order of sentences in first citation altered.

[11] *World as Will and Idea* (Eng. tr.), I, 163.

In this cognition "each of us knows his own nature (*Wesen*) immediately, apart from all form, even that of subject and object—knows and at the same time *is* that which he knows, since here the knower and the known are identical." "Philosophy," Schopenhauer writes again, "necessarily requires that which is absolutely immediate for its starting-point. But clearly only that which is given in self-consciousness fulfills this condition—that which is within and subjective."[12] So Coleridge, following his German originals, writes in the *Biographia Literaria* of "the sacred power of self-intuition" which he equates with "the philosophical imagination."[13]

But this intuiting of the self must not be construed to mean that what is ordinarily understood by introspection—the observation of our fleeting and chaotic contents of consciousness, our sensations, concepts, desires, motives, moods—is the path which leads to the *arcana* of metaphysics. Such introspection at best acquaints us only with what, in Kantian terminology, was called the empirical Ego; and the true Self is, for the metaphysician in one phase of this tendency, the complete antithesis of this empirical self. Novalis was only expressing a commonplace when he wrote: *Unser*

[12] *Ibid.*, I, 145; III, 59.
[13] *Op. cit.* (Shawcross ed.), I, 167.

*sogenanntes Ich ist nicht unser wahres Ich, sondern nur sein Abglanz.*[14] And the "true self" can be *known* only *by* itself.

This limitation of the reality known through the *Vernunft* or "intuition of Reason" to *Das Ich*—to the individual Self *quâ* knower—was not derived from the teaching of Jacobi, and was not approved by him. Though he was the first to formulate the primary article of the creed of the new epistemology—*i.e.*, the distinction of the Reason and the Understanding and the affirmation of the exclusive potency of the former to give us knowledge of the true nature of "reality" —he believed that man possesses a genuine and indubitable knowledge, not only of his own existence and nature, but also of the existence of God, of a physical world, and of the freedom of the human will. There was thus, almost at the outset, a splitting of the new theory of knowledge into two divergent doctrines as to what can be known with certainty through intuition. How this cleavage came about, and what its consequences were, can be understood only after we have considered the question with which the following section will deal.

[14] "Our so called Ego is not our true Ego, but only its reflection." *Fragmente in Schriften.* For the same in Schelling, see *System des transc. Idealismus, SW*, III, 375.

3.   But why do the new epistemologists insist that self-knowledge is the only true knowledge of reality? As the last-cited passage from Schopenhauer implies, the answer—or a part of the answer—is that it seems to them evident that any certain knowledge must be direct, unmediated, an actual *possession* by the knower of that which is known. The sacred word from Jacobi to Bergson and LeRoy has been "immediacy," *das Unmittelbare;* and it was primarily because self-intuition seemed equivalent to immediate knowledge, a direct "acquaintance with" *being*, while the Understanding could at most profess only to yield "knowledge about" it, that the former was given the higher place. "Ever since the time of Aristotle," wrote Jacobi, "there has been going on in the philosophical schools an increasing endeavor to subject immediate knowledge to mediate, the original and fundamental faculty of intuiting or perceiving to the faculty of reflection, which operates by abstraction—to subject the model to its copy, the reality to the verbal symbol, the Reason to the Understanding."[15] By the "immediacy" of intuition these epistemologists did not ordinarily mean the self-evidence of axiomatic propositions, such as were supposed to constitute the foundations of the common logic and of mathematics. For such "abstract fundamental principles" (*Grundsätze*) Schelling has noth-

[15] *Einleitung* to vol. II of Jacobi's *Werke* (1815).

ing but scorn; to place these, he says, "at the summit
of philosophy is the death of philosophy."[16] For
"principles" are generalities, combinations of general
concepts; but a generality is never a fact of immediate
experience, and conceptual thought is the very negation of immediacy; the concept gets in the way of the
reality to be known. No idea *of* anything gives you the
*existence* of that of which it is supposed to be the idea;
for the idea, by hypothesis, is not, and does not contain, the *being* of that which it is said to represent;
nor can it offer any full assurance that it is even a
correct representation of the properties of that entity-
other-than-itself to which it refers.

Now this is, of course, an old *motif* in philosophy
from Descartes to the Scottish School and on to the
now not-so-new realists of our own day.[17] The demand
for immediacy—for the *direct* and therefore sure ap-

---

[16] *SW*, 1, I, 243 (1796).

[17] When he is dealing with the problem of sense-perception,
Schelling, like Jacobi, sometimes under the influence of this
preconception, uses language which might be adopted by a
neo-realist; *e.g.:* "The sound understanding remains, in spite
of everything, unshaken in its belief that the presented object
is at the same time the object in itself; and even the academic
philosopher, as soon as he turns back to actual life, forgets the
whole distinction between phenomena and things in themselves.
. . . It can be historically shown that the prime source of all
scepticism is the notion that there is an original object outside
of us of which the [perceptual] object is merely the effect"
(*SW*, 1, II, 377–78, 17).

prehension of what is known—has been a persistent craving among modern epistemologists—not to say, the sin that doth most easily beset them. Thus the epistemology which we are now considering, in this characteristic of it, is a variety of a familiar genus. But it applies immediacy as the criterion of true knowing in a more rigorous and consistent way than do other species of that genus. Genuinely to know anything you must *be* it—must know it from the inside and not from the outside. In short, the knower (or the knowing act) and the known, subject and object, must be one; and it seemed obvious that only in self-consciousness can this requirement be satisfied. In this alone we *experience* being, and find reality by being real. Upon this theme Schelling dwells with tedious iteration in his writings of 1795 and his *System of Transcendental Idealism* of 1800. Only the existence of the Self (as Descartes saw, without seeing the true implications of this insight) is beyond the reach of doubt, since here the object of the thought is identical with the thinking, and the thinking is its own evidence of its existence:

> I am! My Ego includes a being that is antecedent (*vorhergeht*) to all other thinking and representing. It is, because it is thought, and it is thought because it is; therefore, because it is, and is thought

only in so far as it thinks itself. . . . *Ich bin, weil ich bin!*[18]

This, then, is the "absolute form of knowledge." For such a knowledge

must be a knowing, the object of which is not independent of it, consequently a knowing which produces its own object—an intuition which is freely productive and *in which that which produces and that which is produced are one and the same.* Such an intuition is termed an intellectual intuition in contrast with the intuition of the senses, in which the intuiting is different from the thing intuited. Such an intuition is the Ego because the Ego itself (as object) first comes into being through the knowing of the Ego.

Schopenhauer, who usually found reasons for disagreeing with Schelling when he could, is explicitly in agreement with him in making this immediatism the basic principle of his theory of knowledge.

Manifestly, it is more correct to teach that the world is to be understood through [knowing] man rather than man through [knowing] the world; for it is from that which is given *immediately*, therefore, in self-consciousness, that what is mediately given, *i.e.*, externally perceived, is to be explained.

Jacobi, however, as we have seen, sometimes drew back from this complete identification of the object of

[18] *Vom Ich, usw.; SW,* 1, I, 167.

intuition with *das Ich*. For *his* intuition assured him of the existence both of an external world and of a personal God in certain important senses "external" to the human self. Yet he too liked to dilate upon the ineffably intimate "presence" of God in such intuitional experience.[19] And even for Jacobi the intuition of our own freedom[20]—which intuition is identical with *being* free—is the typical example of immediate knowledge. It was this that Fichte recognized when he wrote enthusiastically to Jacobi: "We are in complete agreement. You too look for all truth where I also look for it: in the innermost sanctuary of our own nature."[21]

This direct apprehension of the Self, Friedrich Schlegel observed, is not the same as having a conception of the Self; it is, in truth, "the certainty of something inconceivable," *i.e.*, of that of which there can be no concept, *die Gewissheit eines Unbegreiflichen;* it is better described as a feeling than as a thought:

> The Ego always eludes us when we seek to fix upon it. The feeling (*das Gefühl*) of this inconceivable is, however, infinitely certain; that is to say, that is certain which one knows immediately, of which no higher proof exists; and that is the case

[19] Cf. *Werke*, II, 119 (*cf.* also *ibid.*, p. 625).
[20] Cf. *Werke*, II, 318.
[21] Letter of April 26, 1796.

with consciousness. This cannot further be deduced
or proved; it is the ground of everything else, is
therefore immediate, absolutely certain. . . . We
shall henceforth always call self-consciousness
*Empfindung*, as a *finding-in-oneself* (*ein-in-sich-
finden*), because the Ego can, properly speaking,
not be proved, but only be found.[22]

Coleridge, it need hardly be recalled, devoted some
twenty consecutive pages of *Biographia Literaria* to
a transcription—in part a literal translation—of
Schelling's reasonings on this theme (though without
mention of their source!).

We are to seek . . . for some absolute truth capable
of communicating to other positions a certainty
which it has not itself borrowed; a truth self-
grounded, unconditional and known by its own
light. In short, we have to find a somewhat which *is*,
simply because it is. In order to be such, it must be
one which is its own predicate. . . . This principle
. . .manifests itself in the SUM or I AM; which I
shall hereafter indiscriminately express by the
words spirit, self and self-consciousness. In this,
and in this alone, object and subject, being and
knowing, are identical. . . . During the act of
knowledge itself, the objective and subjective are so
instantly united that we cannot determine to which

[22] *Philosophische Vorlesungen* (ed. Windischmann), II, 15.
The passage cited does not, of course, express Schlegel's final
doctrine.

the priority belongs. There is here no first and no second; both are coinstantaneous and one.[23]

In the *Anima Poetae* he too finds the identity of the immediate object with the "self" best exemplified in feeling:

> I think of the wall. Here I necessarily think of the idea and the thinking *I* as two distinct and opposite things. Now let me think of myself, of the thinking being. The idea becomes dim—so dim that I scarcely know what it is; but the feeling is deep and steady, and this I call *I*—identifying the percipient and the perceived.

This demand for immediacy in knowledge, the complete unity of knower and known, is equally fundamental in the philosophy of Bergson. In his *Introduction to Metaphysics*, for example, he distinguishes "two profoundly different ways of knowing a thing. The first implies that we move round an object, the second that we enter into it." The former he calls "relative," the latter "absolute" knowledge. A novelist or a biographer seeks to make me "know" his hero's character. He may, by multiplying incidents,

[23] *Op. cit.*, ch. XII, pp. 181 f., 174. The last two sentences quoted are taken verbatim from the opening page of Schelling's *System of Transcendental Idealism: Im Wissen selbst ist Objektives und Subjektives so vereint, dass man nicht sagen kann, welchem von beiden die Priorität zukomme. Es ist hier kein Erstes und kein Zweites, beide sind gleichzeitig und Eins.*

descriptions, analyses, tell me much *about* the hero; but—writes Bergson—"all this can never be equivalent to the simple and indivisible feeling which I should experience if I were able for an instant to identify myself with the person of the hero himself." "That which is properly himself, that which constitutes his essence, cannot be perceived from without." Imaginative sympathy may perhaps achieve some approximation to it. But metaphysics discloses to us "a means of *possessing* a reality absolutely instead of *knowing* it relatively, of placing oneself within it instead of looking at it from outside points of view, of having the intuition instead of making the analysis." And, of course, this "reality which we can thus seize from within . . . is our own personality in its flowing through time—our enduring self."[24]

A philosophy which thus bases itself solely upon what is immediately given stands, Bergson insists, on a wholly different footing from all other philosophies:

Is it asserted that this manner of envisaging concepts [as merely tools for action] is simply a philosophical theory, and that this theory is neither better nor worse than other theories? I reply that the immediate is its own justification and has its value in itself, independently of this theory of the

[24] *Op. cit.*, pp. 1–9 and *passim*; italics mine.

concept. In fact, all philosophies which limit the scope of the immediate are necessarily in conflict with one another, being merely so many views taken of the immediate by placing oneself at different points of view—by taking aim at it with different categories.

But when we come back to the immediate in its actual immediacy—not as a sort of target to be shot at from the outside—all the conflicts between philosophical theories disappear, with the disappearance of the problems which give rise to them.

Each of these philosophies, when one places oneself at the point of view of one of the others, appears as a source of contradictions and insoluble difficulties. On the contrary, the return to the immediate removes the contradictions and oppositions, by dissipating the problem about which the combat arose. This power of the immediate—I mean its capacity to resolve oppositions by suppressing problems—is, in my opinion, the external mark by which the true intuition of the immediate may be recognized.[25]

To a consideration of the potency claimed for the immediate in the last sentence we shall have to return at a later point; for the present, the passage is pertinent simply as an especially clear expression of the

[25] Bergson's note on the article "Immédiat" in Lalande's *Vocabulaire de la Philosophie* (1928), I, 349.

fundamental place of immediatism in Bergson's doctrine.

4. The identification of knowledge with a sort of immediate experience has often led these epistemologists to adopt a fashion of speech which sounds like that of scientific empiricism. Since the "intuition" was conceived, not as the recognition of the truth of a general proposition, but, after the analogy of sense-perception, as the direct apprehension of a concrete datum, the philosophy based upon this intuition professed to be a simple report of empirical facts; and it assumed that tone of condescension towards "mere reasoning" and "dialectic" which empiricists have usually held. Thus, according to Jacobi (as one of his contemporaries of Schellingian affiliations expressed it):

> Of actual existence there are not two kinds of knowledge, an *a priori* and an *a posteriori*, but only one, the *a posteriori*, through sensation (*Empfindung*). And since all knowledge which does not arise *a priori* is faith, therefore all real knowledge depends upon faith, since things must first be *given* before one is in a position to apprehend relations between them.[26]

[26] T. A. Rixner, in his *Handbuch der Gesch. der Philosophie* (1823), III, 319. The terms Rixner here uses are equivalent in

But this so-called faith is not an inferior sort of knowledge, but rather a knowledge at first hand, "infinitely better and less deceptive than that deduced by demonstrative reasoning, and yielding a *perception* of the super-sensible." "It is not a science or kind of knowledge either capable of, or in need of, proof." Schelling repeats and accentuates this remark in 1795:

> From experience, from immediate experience, must all our knowledge come: this is a truth which has already been expressed by many philosophers, who fell short of the whole truth of the matter only in that they failed to make clear the nature of this intuition [or perception]. From experience, indeed; but—since all experience which refers to *objects* is mediated through another—from an experience *immediate* in the strictest sense of the word, an experience that is self-produced and independent of all external causality, must our knowledge be derived.[27]

Somewhat in this spirit Friedrich Schlegel wrote in one of the *Athenaeumsfragmente:*

"Demonstrations" in philosophy are merely demonstrations in the sense which the word has in tech-

Jacobi's early writings to the *Vernunft* and *Anschauung* of his later period.

[27] *SW*, 1 Abt., I, p. 318: *Philosophische Briefe, usw.;* italics in the original.

nical military language [*i.e.*, displays, parades].
. . . They have their purpose and value as attesta-
tions of competency and proofs of virtuosity, like
the *bravura* passages of a singer, or the use of Latin
by philologists. And they have no small rhetorical
effectiveness. But the main thing, after all, is merely
that a man should *know* something and should say
it. To prove it or even explain it is in most cases
wholly superfluous. . . . The categorical style of the
Decalogue remains the most suitable even to the
most subtle *Naturphilosophie* . . . Leibniz affirmed
and Wolff proved: enough said.[28]

It is amusing to find Schopenhauer reproaching
his immediate precursors for their ignorance of this
idea, in a passage in which he is plainly engaged in
filching the idea from them.

A strange and unsuitable definition of philosophy
—which Kant, nevertheless, has presented—is this,
that it is a knowledge from mere concepts (*aus
blossen Begriffen*). In truth, concepts possess nothing except what has been put into them after it has
first been begged or borrowed from intuitive [or
perceptual, *anschaulich*] experience, that true and
inexhaustible source of all insight. Consequently
a true philosophy cannot be spun out from mere
abstract concepts, but must be grounded on observation and experience, inner and outer. Not
through experiments in the combination of con-

[28] *Fragmente* (1798), in *Athenaeum*, I, 2, p. 21.

cepts, such as have been carried out so often, especially by the sophists of our own time—by Fichte and Schelling, and in the most deplorable fashion of all by Hegel, and in the domain of ethics by Schleiermacher—not in such a way can anything be rightly accomplished in philosophy. Philosophy must, like art and poetry, have its source in the intuitive apprehension of the world (*in der anschaulichen Auffassung der Welt*).[29]

The same type of phraseology recurs in Bergson. He is given to remarking that there is a sense in which the method of an intuitional philosophy is identical with the method of positive science. Both, namely, are strictly empirical. The author of the *Essai sur les données immédiates de la conscience* delighted to represent himself, not as a subtle dialectician, but as merely a faithful reporter of observed—but inwardly observed—facts.[30] All that is not the pure and simple statement of a fact (*la constatation pure et simple des faits*) he desires to avoid; there is to be no admixture of mere inference and ratiocination in his teaching. "The philosophic method, as I understand it," he writes to Father de Tonquédec, "is rigorously moulded upon experience (inner or outer) and does

[29] *Parerga und Paralipomena*, "Ueber Philosophie und ihre Methode" (Eng. tr., Bohn), sec. 9, p. 168.

[30] No one, of course, can read many pages of Bergson and continue to regard this representation as lifelike.

not permit one to enunciate a conclusion which in any measure goes beyond the considerations upon which it is based. If my works have been able to inspire some confidence in minds which philosophy had hitherto left indifferent, it is for this reason: I have never given any place to what was simply a personal opinion, or a conviction incapable of being objectified by this particular method."[31]

5. The immediatism which has been illustrated in the two preceding sections may, to the non-philosophical reader, seem only a highly abstract and technical—and also a highly obscure—epistemological theorem. But it helped to produce in some of the writers affected by this way of thinking a rather characteristic moral and aesthetic temper—an antipathy or, at the least, a professed antipathy, to all that is *secondhand* in life, thought, and art. Nothing is really valid for a man except what he has himself inwardly and intimately experienced. The bare intellectual apprehension of a truth (*i.e.*, of a relation between general concepts), especially if it be a truth merely learned from someone else, is not enough; for thinking or reasoning *about* things is never equivalent

[31] *Les Études, publiés par les Peres de la Société de Jésus* (1912).

to direct experiencing. This idea easily passed over into, or was confused with, an emphasis on intensity or energy of feeling as a mark of the true intuitive apprehension of the "real"; for feeling seems a more immediate and internal and personal experience than thinking. When you feel, the feeling, as we have seen Coleridge intimating, is *you*, not a dubious image of something else external to you.

Thus Schelling liked to reiterate that reality must be lived, not thought:

> One who does not know anything *real* within him and outside of him—who does but play with concepts and lives only by concepts—whose faculty of intuition has been killed through the substitution of memorizing for immediate experience (*durch Gedächtniswerk*) or through the corrupting influence of society—one to whom his own existence is nothing more than a languid thought—how, pray, can such a one speak of reality? It is *as* if a blind man should talk about colors.[32]

And again, connecting this idea with some of the themes which we have earlier noted:

> A philosophy which is grounded upon the essential nature of man himself cannot resort to lifeless formulas—so many prisons for the human spirit— nor to labored artifices of philosophizing, which do

[32] *SW.*, 1, I, 353.

but . . . bury the living functioning of the human mind in dead faculties. It rather, if I may borrow an expression of Jacobi's, has for its aim to unveil and reveal *Existence (Dasein)*. . . . Its spirit and essence, therefore, . . . its highest object, must be, not something mediated through concepts nor laboriously put together into concepts, but that *in* man which is immediately present to himself alone.[33]

*Philosophiren*, wrote Novalis in the same spirit, *ist dephlegmatisiren, vivificiren.* "Hitherto philosophers in their inquiries have first put philosophy to death and then dismembered it. Only in the most recent times has a beginning been made at studying philosophy alive."[34]

Thus the word "life"—in a sense difficult to determine except that it implies a contrast with the intellectual functions, with all the reflective processes in which philosophy had usually been supposed to consist—became another of the sacred words of these philosophers. Even Fichte, in a fragment of 1799, went so far as to set up a formal antithesis between "life" and "philosophizing" in the traditional sense: "To live is, distinctively, not to philosophize, to philosophize is, distinctively, not to live. (*Leben ist ganz eigentlich Nichtphilosophiren; Philosophiren ist*

[33] *Vom Ich, usw.; SW*, 1, I, 156.
[34] *Schriften*, 5te Aufl., II, 113.

*ganz eigentlich Nichtleben*); and I know of no more apt way of defining the two conceptions than this. There is here a perfect antithesis."[35] Fichte, however, adds that though the two "standpoints" cannot be unified, the philosopher must nevertheless try to place himself in both. It was more characteristic of German thinkers of Schellingian sympathies to say that the new and true philosophy, precisely because it was an escape from the devitalizing Understanding, was a return to, a rediscovery of, "life."

Here again Bergson repeats the same strain. To philosophize, for him, is (ostensibly) not to reflect *about* life, but to abandon the reflective or external attitude, and thus to *live* more intensely and directly than can those who have not been emancipated through the discovery of the inadequacy of the intellect. For, in Bergson's own phrase, intelligence is characterized by a natural inability to comprehend the living (*l'intelligence est caractérisée par une incompréhension naturelle de la vie*).[36] "So long"—writes one of his disciples, E. LeRoy—"So long as you insist upon seeking the object outside itself—where it certainly is not—how shall you ever discover its inward reality and its distinctive essence? . . . The philosopher

[35] In Fichte's *Leben und literarischer Briefwechsel* (1862), II, 174–75.

[36] *L'évolution créatrice* (1907), p. 308; English tr., p. 165.

should take an attitude exactly the reverse of all this: should not keep at a distance from things, but . . . should make that effort of sympathy by which one places oneself within the object, merges oneself to its rhythm and—in one word—*lives* it." But this is the complete antithesis to what philosophers call "conceptual analysis, the attempt to resolve all reality into general notions."[37]

6. It may, however, well seem that we ourselves have thus far hardly discovered what the intellectual intuition is "from within." For we have been given little more than external and negative characterizations of it, in somewhat general terms.

[37] E. LeRoy, *Une philosophie nouvelle* (1912), pp. 35–39. In his later work, *La pensée primitive* (1929), LeRoy, distinguishing the *données immédiates* or *données primitives*, which are *vécues* rather than *conçues*, from all reflective and practical thought, declares that "our task is to return to these [the immediate data] as much as possible in order to equalize ever more and more *notre intelligence claire à notre perception primordiale*." To say this, however—he insists—is "not to fail to recognize the sovereign and universal rôle of thought"; it is only "to distinguish between the intuitive and the discursive function of the mind; the latter should be adjusted to (*se régler sur*) the former." Just how this recognizes "the sovereign and universal role of thought" I am unable to understand; but I quote the words as indicating that the citation in the text may not express precisely LeRoy's later position.

We have been told several things *about* it: that it is an "immediate" kind of knowing; that it is therefore wholly different from conceptual thought, but is more akin to feeling or to sensation; that it is not, however, a sensing of the physical qualities of external objects, but is a knowing of our own "inner" or "deeper" self. But since these epistemologists insist that it is a special kind of *experience*, and also that it cannot be communicated by verbal descriptions, it would seem that, if he is to introduce us, the uninitiated, to it, he should either tell us what we must do to get this experience, or—if it be something that we have already had without realizing its import—should *point* to those moments or phases of experience in which it is exemplified. The philosophers of the ineffable have usually taken the former course; they have told us through what discipline or propaedeutic the soul may be made ready to receive the saving knowledge; thus Plato bids us study mathematics and practise austerity of life, and the mystics, however inexpressible they have recognized the ultimate experience of "union" with the divine to be, have often been explicit enough in enumerating the stages of approach to it.

Now, if we ask one of these epistemologists to point us to the experience which *is* the intuition, or at least to show us the road to it, we sometimes get a very curious answer. We have seen that, according to his doctrine, we apprehend the inner self in the degree in which we turn away from the external world and from the practical business of our sensible existence. It should apparently follow that we are nearer to an "immediate unintellectualized possession" of the deep-lying Ego in sleep than in waking life. And Schelling does not fail to note this implication, though he does not much care for it, and for the most part keeps it in the background. In sleep, he observes, though the senses are stilled, the soul cannot be wholly unconscious but must continue in some way to produce representations.

> But so long as the soul is thus freed from the body, and thereby all relation to external space becomes impossible to it—in this condition the soul sees everything only *within* itself; nothing in it takes the form of a concept or a judgment.[38]

But just this "seeing everything within oneself," without the intrusion of the "forms of conception or judgment" should be for Schelling precisely—the *intellektuelle Anschauung*.

To this possible way of construing the "intuition" corresponded that preoccupation with sleep, dream,

[38] *SW*, 1 Abt., I, *Abhandlungen zur Erlauterung des Idealismus der Wissenschaftslehre* . . . written in 1796–7—referred to hereafter as "Abhandlungen," p. 391. Cf. also *SW*, 1, III, 506–507.

somnambulism, and revery which is characteristic of many writers of what is often called the German Romantic Period. All of them, the French author of a psychological study of Novalis has remarked (with some exaggeration), were, or believed themselves to be, endowed in some degree with "a spontaneous intuition which has its locus in the inner faculty of dreaming," (*une spontanéité d'intuition, qui a primitivement son siège dans l'organe intérieur du rêve*)[39] Novalis, for example, and J. W. Ritter, conceived that "in the state of trance or autohypnotic sleep they had discovered a condition of 'will-lessness' (*Unwillkür*) in which the soul attains a pure intuition of the Absolute. The consciousness of a man in this condition of *Unwillkür* (. . . the 'intellectual intuition')— of a man, in other words, who is in a hypnotic sleep— thus becomes the key of knowledge."[40] Tieck writes in the same vein in *William Lovell* (1795–96):

[39] E. Spenlé, in his Novalis: *Essai sur l'idealisme romantique en Allemagne* (1903), p. 155. Cf. also A. Beguin, *L'Ame romantique et le Rêve* (1937).

[40] Walzel, *Deutsche Romantik* (1912), pp. 45 ff.; cf. the same work, pp. 139–40. But on the other hand, Novalis elsewhere writes: "Sleep is a suspension of the higher faculties—a withdrawal of the intellectual impulsion—the impulsion which is supposed to be absolute" (*Schlummer ist ein Anhalten des höheren Organs—eine Entziehung des geistigen Reitzes—des absolut seyn sollenden Reitzes*). (*Schriften*, [1901], II, 1, p. 135).

Perhaps dreams are our highest philosophy. Perhaps we are to experience a great revelation which will accomplish at one stroke what reason must forever fail to accomplish: a solution of all mysteries, both those within and those without us. Perhaps all illusion will vanish when we reach a height of vision which to the rest of mankind seems the height of absurdity.

While Brandes goes too far when he describes the dream-state as "the ideal of German Romanticism,"[41] he would have kept within the truth if he had said that it was *one* of the ideals of many writers of the so-called Romantic period; and the writers who most explicitly treated it as such, it is evident, were in harmony with one—though a decidedly minor—strain in Schelling's philosophy.

In Schopenhauer we find it affirmed clearly enough that the Will—which is to say, the true nature of our own being and of the universal life—is more clearly revealed in the sleeping than in the waking state. "Nothing," he writes, "proves more clearly the secondary, dependent, conditioned nature of the intellect than its periodical intermittence."

In deep sleep all knowledge and forming of ideas ceases. But the kernel of our nature, the metaphysical part of it which the organic functions necessarily

[41] *The Romantic School in Germany*, p. 15.

presuppose as their *primum mobile,* must never pause, if life is not to cease. . . . In sleep, when only the vegetative life is carried on, the Will works only according to its original and essential nature, undisturbed from without, with no diminution of its power through the activity of the intellect.

But nothing could well be more boldly in conflict than this inverted inference with the prevailing tendency of Schopenhauer's reasoning, at least in his earlier and better-known writings. For he ordinarily tells us that it is the intellect which spreads the veil of *Māyā* before the face of reality and thus is the source of all the evil of existence.

It is similarly an implication of Bergson's account of the relation of intuition to the intellect that the type of ordinary experience which approximates his much-extolled intuition is none other than sleep—or at least, dream. For in this state the mind is relatively, though even yet not absolutely withdrawn into itself; it is freed from the exigencies of action, and its points of contact with the material world in which action takes place are obstructed. And since the intuition consists in a complete withdrawal into the inner self, and demands a complete freedom from the preoccupations of the active life, it must be to that condition, or at least to an approximation to it, that we attain in our dreaming life. This implication has been little noted by Bergson's commentators; yet it cannot be said to be a tacit one. On the contrary, it is explicitly drawn out in his earliest book. We are there told that the true experience of "duration," which for most of us in our waking hours is habitually falsified by the intrusion into it of spatial forms and quantitative categories, is attained by all of us in sleep:

> That our ordinary conception of duration depends on a gradual incursion of space into the domain of pure consciousness is proved by the fact that in order to deprive the Ego of the faculty of perceiving a homogeneous [*i.e.*, a spatialized and therefore "denatured"] time, it is enough to take away from it this outer circle of psychic states which it uses as a balance-wheel. These conditions are realized when we dream; for sleep, by relaxing the play of the organic functions, alters the communicating surface between the Ego and external objects. Here we no longer measure duration, but feel it; from quantity it returns to the state of quality; we no longer estimate past time mathematically.[42]

The reader of these words must remember that, throughout the work from which they are taken, just this result—the return to "pure duration," the purgation of consciousness from all ideas of number and measure, the apprehension of it as "quality" with no

[42] *Time and Free Will* (Eng. tr., London, 1910), pp. 126–27.

element of "quantity" is held up as the consummation most to be desired by those who would attain philosophical insight. Throughout *Matter and Memory,* also, the same implication is writ large for all who can put two propositions together and recognize their joint import. For there too we are shown, on the one hand, how, through the demands of the life of action, consciousness, which in its genuine character is pure and complete memory, gets deformed into sense-perception in a series of supposed "present" and instantaneous moments, of which transformation our bodily mechanism is a sort of expression; and we are told, on the other hand, that "in deep sleep we have at least a functional break in the nervous system between stimulation and motor-reaction, so that dreams would be the state of a mind of which the attention was not fixed by the sensori-motor equilibrium of the body."[43] In short, on "the plane of dream" we have pure memory; but, according to the doctrine of the volume in question, "pure recollection is already spirit," whereas external perception "is in a sense matter." But the business of philosophy (though not of science or practical life) is with spirit rather than matter; its concern is to know consciousness in its primal purity, not in its functional metamorphoses or disguises. Hence it should follow that a

[43] *Matter and Memory* (Eng. tr., London, 1911), p. 228.

method, if not *the* method, of philosophizing is to dream. As Bergson has elsewhere declared:

> The dream state is the substratum of our normal state. Nothing is added in waking life; on the contrary, waking life is obtained by the limitation, concentration and tension of that diffuse psychic life which is the dreaming life. . . . The dreaming ego is less *tense,* but more *extended,* than the waking ego.[44]

How hardly, then, shall they that are awake possess that intuition of *le moi profond* through which alone philosophical insight is attained!

All this, then, is an unmistakable part of the Bergsonian doctrine of the nature of intuition. But it is, of course, a part of which the significance seems seldom fully realized by the author of the doctrine, one of those which he oftenest forgets, and, indeed, as we shall see, sometimes expressly contradicts. One of the ablest of Bergson's disciples, Segond, has noted this apparent implication, but endeavors to show that it is only apparent. "It is true," he writes, "that our misapprehensions of the real and of becoming are due to our employing for purposes of thought the forms of action. . . . And if dream, which is foreign to action, reestablishes between things the continuity which action abolishes, ought we not to seek in it the

[44] *Revue philosophique* (December, 1908), p. 574.

faithful image of that pure knowledge which eludes the forms of our practical thinking?"[45] To justify his finally negative answer to this question, Segond observes that "in this dream-knowledge there are lacking the effort of volition and the intelligent orientation of our personal memories which that effort makes possible." Precisely; but, on Bergsonian principles, they ought to be lacking. Segond appears determined to regard pure intuition and intellect, the form of "speculation" and the form of action, as equally fundamental in Bergson's account of the method of metaphysical insight. But if there is anything which Bergson plainly repudiates, it is the supposition that the two can possibly be equally fundamental or equally valuable. If he had not disregarded this fact, Segond would have been compelled to answer his question in the affirmative.

This, however, is not the heart of the mystery for these philosophers; they were not, after all, chiefly preachers of a gospel of philosophic salvation through somnolence, and the intuition of the deeper self did not consist merely in a state of consciousness in which the activity of the bodily senses is reduced to a minimum. The essence and the value of the intuition were conceived, above all—in the phase of the doctrine with which we are just now concerned—to lie in the

[45] *L'intuition Bergsonienne* (3rd ed., 1930), pp. 98–99.

fact that that experience was regarded as an escape from the limitations and frustrations of time—at least of time as we commonly think of it. This, however, is so large, important, and involved a topic that it must be dealt with in another lecture.

# Lecture III

Time as ordinarily conceived is sundered into separate moments which are perpetually passing away. The past is forever dead and gone, the future is non-existent and uncertain, and the present seems, at most, a bare knife-edge of existence separating these two unrealities, itself scarcely born before it also lapses into nonentity. To many reflective minds in all ages time, so conceived, has seemed a baffling, unintelligible, incredible mode of being, undeserving of the eulogistic epithet of "real," or at all events, not the final and universal attribute of the nature of things. Like Aldous Huxley's Mr. Propter, thousands of weary souls have found time to be a "thing *intrinsically* nightmarish."[1] A great part of the history of Western, as of Eastern, philosophy, therefore, has been a persistent flight from the temporal to the eternal, the quest of an object on which the reason or the imagination might fix itself with the sense of having attained to something that is not merely perduring but immutable, because the very notions of "before"

[1] *After Many a Summer Dies the Swan* (1939), p. 117.

and "after" are inapplicable to it. And of this quest
the theory of knowledge under consideration is, on
one side, a phase—though, as we shall later see, on
another side it is precisely the opposite. But these
philosophers sought the object of the quest, like the
Blue Bird, at home—not in the remote world of
Platonic Ideas or Realm of Essence, nor in a transcendent Aristotelian God, nor—as Spenser does, in
the *locus classicus* of this theme in English poetry,
the cantos on Mutability with which *The Faerie
Queene* ends—in a future eternal Sabbath to which
we may aspire:

> That time . . . when no more *Change* shall be
> But stedfast rest of all things finally stayd
> Upon the pillours of Eternity,
> That is contrayr to *Mutabilitie:*
> For all that moveth, doth in *Change* delight:
> But henceforth all shall rest eternally
> With Him that is the God of Sabbaoth hight:
> O! that great Sabbaoth God, grant me that Sab-
> baoth's sight.[2]

Spenser's "eternity" differed profoundly—as was to
be expected from a poet reared in the tradition of
Christian philosophy—from the timelessness of

[2] *The Works of Edmund Spenser, Variorum Edition: The
Faerie Queene, Books Six and Seven* (1938), p. 181. Spenser,
being presumably ignorant of Hebrew, had, of course, confused
the word meaning "hosts" or "armies" (*Numbers* 4, *passim;
Romans* 9:29) with that meaning "rest."

Plato's Idea or Aristotle's God; the poet's lines were the expression of a hope for the future attainment by individual human souls of a state of being exempt from mutability—which for him (as for Dante) probably meant a changeless beatific contemplation of the perfection—itself eternal—of the Supreme Being.

Eternity, on the contrary, the philosophers here in question often declare, is already within us; for the Self known directly in intuition is a pure unity, an existence in which there are no parts external to one another, as are—or seem to be—the successive instants of time. Thus Schelling writes:

> Because the Ego is indivisible, it is likewise incapable of change. For it cannot be changed by anything external. But if it were self-changed, it would be necessary that one part of it should be determined by another, *i.e.*, it would be divisible. The Ego, therefore, must be always the same, an absolute unity placed beyond the reach of all mutation. . . . One cannot say of it: it was, it will be; but only *it is*. . . . The form of the intellectual intuition of it is eternity.[3]

[3] *SW*, 1 Abt., I, *Vom Ich als Princip der Philosophie* (1795), pp. 192–202. So in *System des transc. Idealismus* (*SW*, 1, III, 396): It is *through* self-consciousness that all limitation, and so also all time, arises; that original activity, therefore, cannot fall within time; the Ego as Ego is absolutely eternal; i.e., outside of time altogether (*das Ich als ich ist absolut ewig, d. h. ausser aller Zeit*).

At this point the Schellingian and the Kantian forms of the doctrine of two faculties of knowledge coincide, or at least overlap. For Kant's noumenal Ego—the reality of which, unknown to the theoretical Understanding, the Practical Reason reveals—belongs, as we have seen, to the "intelligible" world, in the Platonistic sense, and has as little to do with time as with space. But for Schelling this transcendence of temporal existence is neither a postulate nor merely a deduction from a metaphysical axiom; it is an experience. In its immediate awareness of itself the Ego *knows* eternity at first hand, and lives in the eternal. In setting forth the delights of this experience Schelling rises to a nebulous eloquence:

> In all of us there dwells a mysterious and wonderful power to withdraw ourselves from the changes of time into our innermost self, freed from all that comes to us from without, and to intuit the eternal in us under the form of immutability. This intuition is the most inward and the most individual of experiences, upon which alone depends all that we know and believe of a supersensible world. . . . This intellectual intuition appears, then, when we cease to be an *object* to ourselves; when, withdrawn into itself, the intuiting self is identical with the intuited. In this moment of intuition time and duration vanish for us; we are no longer in time but time is in us—or rather, *not* time, but pure, absolute eternity.

We are not *in* the intuition of the objective world, but that world is lost in our intuition. . . . This principle—of intuition and experience—alone can breathe the breath of life into the lifeless system [of things]; even the most abstract concepts with which our knowledge plays depends upon an experience *die auf Leben und Dasein geht,* which takes hold upon life and existence itself.[4]

Characteristic is the recurrence here of the blessed word "life" and the insistence that the intuition is a sort of heightening of the feeling of vitality; but this "life" is now identified, *not* with any process or activity in time, but is just—eternity.

We find Novalis similarly declaring that the self's discovery of itself is also a discovery of that in which the parts of time are fused into a unity: "in ourselves, or nowhere, is eternity with its two worlds of past and future."[5] And from this consideration he gains the comforting assurance that, in all our endless temporal striving, we are in reality forever at the goal:

Since our nature, or the plenitude of our essential being (*Wesen*), is infinite, we consequently cannot

[4] *SW*, 1 Abt., I, *Philosophische Briefe über Dogmatismus und Kritizismus* (1795), pp. 318–19. The order of the sentences is in one instance altered in citation.

[5] *Schriften* (1837), p. 4. Cf. a passage in *Die Lehrlinge zu Sais,* "Nothing is so noteworthy as the great simultaneity (*Zugleich*) of Nature. Everywhere Nature seems all present; it is, in the midst of time, past, present and future at once."

reach this goal in time. But since we also exist in a sphere outside of time, we thereby necessarily *do* reach that goal in every moment. . . . In this the spirit can find rest; for an endless striving after the goal, without ever reaching it, seems intolerable.[6]

Schleiermacher, in his first *Monologue*, tells us that in order to attain through self-intuition to the consciousness of what we truly are we must cease to apply to ourselves, as men habitually do, the categories which are in reality made by us and are meant to be applied to *other* objects; and this means, above all, that we must not think of ourselves as living in a divisible time. All our divisions of time are artificial and arbitrary; when we seek ultimately to resolve time into "moments" we find that out of moments no time can be composed. The moments into which we sunder time "are no part of temporal life." In the true Self, all is present at once.

The sensuous man is incapable of thinking of himself as aught but a multiplicity of transitory phenomena, each of which destroys and obliterates its predecessor; the complete picture of his own being is broken up into a thousand incongruous fragments. . . . But in the inner life all is one, every action is only the completion of another, each is contained

[6] *Fragmente*, in *Schriften* (1901 ed.), II, 2, p. 622.

within every other. . . . There is no activity in me which I can rightly regard separately.

He who realizes these truths becomes free from time. "When I return within myself in order to gain the intuition of freedom, my eye is turned away from time's domain."[7]

The same assertion of the indivisibility, and consequently the timelessness and immutability, of that which is the real "essence" of each of us—*i.e.*, "the Will"—is fundamental in Schopenhauer's *Die Welt als Wille und Vorstellung* (in its first edition). "The multiplicity of things in space and time, which constitutes the objectification of the Will, does not affect the Will itself, which remains indivisible notwithstanding it." "The Will reveals itself as completely in one oak as in millions." Apart from its phenomenal forms, the true Will abides in an eternal Now, a *nunc stans*, which, however, embraces all that is absolutely real of what, in the language of the phenomenal world, we call past and future.

We must now, however, note a certain peculiarity of terminology, pertinent to this topic, which Schelling introduced. The immutable mode of being which belongs to the Ego, Schelling sometimes *calls* "time." For he distinguishes two kinds of time—that is, two

[7] *Monologen* (1800), pp. 10–22, *passim*.

senses of the word. There is "absolute" or "pure" time, which is "time in its complete independence of space," and the *idea* of time, in which it is associated with the idea of space. In the former, "the Ego, in the highest state of feeling, has its whole unbounded activity concentrated, as it were, into a single point."[8] "Pure time," in short, consists of the moment. To think of time—as we ordinarily do—as spread out, as a sort of linear extended magnitude, is to introduce into our thought of it the distinctive attribute of space; for space (according to Schelling's analysis of the concept) is pure extensity, *die absolute Extensität,* its differentia is that its parts are all external to one another; while the notion of time is that of absolute "intensity" without extension. In space, which is "the negation of all intensity"—that is, so to say, of all focusing of content into a point—the Ego is "as it were decomposed" (*aufgelöst*);[9] whereas, "in an absolute time nothing must be thought as *auseinander,* as external to anything else (all in one point)."[10] Thus completely despatialized "time" could mean what philosophy had usually meant by eternity.

But, as several passages already cited imply, the

[8] *System des transc. Idealismus; SW*, 1, III, 467.

[9] *Ibid.*

[10] *Ideen zu einer Philosophie der Natur* (1797, 1803); *SW*, 1, II, 231.

temporally unextended or punctual character of the absolute moment in which the Ego experiences its true nature did not mean (at least in the phase of the doctrine which is now under consideration) that it is a moment with nothing in it. The *content* of the successive moments of time, in the ordinary sense, could not be left out of the intuition which transcends time—in that sense. All that the empirical self experiences, whether yesterday, today, or tomorrow, in some sense certainly exists; it is not just nothingness. Time and eternity could perhaps, in a Platonistic scheme of things, remain two contrasted, mutually external realms; but the two *selves* could not be admitted to be so unrelated and independent, since the one—the temporal or phenomenal self—exists for and through the other. In some manner that which has its being in time—that is, in mutually exclusive, successive moments—must be contained in the eternal self, in one indivisible moment; or, conversely, *each* moment of the succession must be eternal, must somehow be conceived as simultaneously comprehending all the reality there is in all the so-called other moments. Into each the entire life of the temporal Ego must be compacted. "Every moment, therefore," says Schelling, in his *Weltseele* (1798), "every moment possesses the same eternity as the whole. For this reason, it is evident that the *Zeitleben,* the temporal life, considered in itself, is not different from the eternal, but is, rather, itself its *eternal being*. . . . In order to understand this, let us present it . . . in the form of a myth. Suppose time to have already run its course, and therefore to be now eternity; and suppose yourself to be now existing in this eternity. But the eternity which you are imagining as time that has run its course, *als abgelaufene Zeit*, already is"—that is, is embraced without succession in the present moment.[11] "Since all time arises through the pure willing and activity of the mind, one can thereby understand also the co-instantaneousness of all things in the world."[12] And this "being-all-at-once," *Zugleichsein*, of the content of the successive experiences of the temporal Ego —however difficult to frame in concepts or to express in words—is the essential nature of that mode of being which the intellectual intuition is (sometimes) declared to reveal.

These ideas of Schelling's seem to have especially aroused the interest of Coleridge, and were reproduced and somewhat amplified by him—though without mention of their source. In the spring of 1801 he went through, as his biographers have usually recognized, a crisis in his mental history, of which he

[11] *SW*, 1, III, 365.
[12] *SW*, 1, I, 397. In the sequel, a quite different turn is given to this conception, with which we shall deal later.

gives some account in a letter to his friend Thomas
Poole. After a period "of the most intense study,"
he reports, he had attained three most important in-
sights; and, first of all, had *"completely extricated the
notions of time and space,"* by which he appears to
mean that he had completely distinguished the one
concept from the other.[13] He does not, in the letter,
explain in what he conceived the distinction to consist;
but the explanation is apparently to be found in passages of *Biographia Literaria,* long after:

> The act of consciousness is indeed identical with
> time considered in its essence. I mean time *per se,*
> as contradistinguished from our notion of time; for
> this is always blended with the idea of space,
> which, as the opposite of time, is therefore its
> measure.[14]

[13] *Letters* (1895 ed.), I, 348; italics in original. On this, see
my "Coleridge and Kant's Two Worlds," *Essays in the History
of Ideas* (1948). It is difficult to believe that this discovery,
which Coleridge represents as his own, was not in fact derived
from certain passages in the *System des transcendentalen
Idealismus,* the work of Schelling's which he seems to have
known best. But—as Sara Coleridge pointed out in defending
him against the charge of conscious plagiarism—he was almost
habitually unable to distinguish ideas which had come to him
from others from those which he had himself excogitated.

[14] *Biogr. Lit.* (ed. Shawcross), I, 187. The conception of space
as the "measure" of time is also to be found in the *Transcendental Idealism* (*SW,* 1, III, 468) where Schelling explains in

Now what *is* "time *per se*," unblended with the idea of space? Coleridge, again characteristically is not at this point explicit; but since the whole passage is pure Schelling, there can be little doubt that he too meant that a completely despatialized time is not "extended," that the moments of it are not, as are the points of space, mutually external, but rather compresent and concentrated into *one* moment. And this, he tells us elsewhere in the same writing, we have empirical reasons to believe that they are, for the true "self" of the individual; if it were not for the material body (which, of course, is conditioned by spatiality) it is "probable" that we should simultaneously apprehend and possess all the experiences which *seem* separated as past and present; that

> it would require only a different and appropriate organization—the *body celestial* instead of the *body terrestrial*—to bring before every human soul the collective experience of its whole past existence. . . . Yea, in the very nature of a living spirit, it may be more possible that heaven and earth should pass away, than that a single act, a single thought, should be loosened or lost from that living chain of causes, with all the links of which, conscious or un-

what sense, and why, this can be said. The Schellingian original of the passage is recognized by Sara Coleridge in her note on it in the 1847 edition of *Biographia Literaria*.

conscious, the free will, our only absolute Self, is co-extensive and co-present.[15]

Nor, indeed, need we wait to attain the "body celestial" to have evidence for this; for there are exceptional but "authenticated" cases of memory—when the subjects are in a "feverish state"—which at least go to show that "all thoughts are imperishable"; and since the physical state can be no more than a stimulus, these cases (such is Coleridge's argument) indicate that, even in this life, to "our absolute Self" every "thought" (*i.e.*, past content of consciousness) is at every moment present.

It is to be observed that, in all this way of thinking, time and eternity have a curious, not to say contradictory, threefold relation. When the Ego is experiencing itself as it truly is, it is asserted to be "outside of time," that is, of divided and successive time; but also, time is in a sense in *it*, inasmuch as all the reality contained in the divided and successive moments of ordinary temporal existence is indivisibly compresent in that instant of experience; and finally, that same experience, with all that it contains, is

[15] *Ibid.*, p. 180. The relation of this idea to Coleridge's doctrine of freedom does not here concern us. It is discussed in the paper, cited in note 13 above, in my *Essays in the History of Ideas* (1948). But it is pertinent at this point to recall that Coleridge's "free will," or "absolute self," was supratemporal.

after all *in* time, since it is declared to be, or to be
capable of being, an empirical event, occurring or
not occurring at a given date in the succession of
mutually external moments constituting the phenomenal life of an individual. As an inferred object
of *belief* or contemplation, no doubt, the "deeper
self" might consistently be said, by these philosophers,
not to be in time, in this last sense. But as a concrete
datum of immediate experience, it is; for the intuition
of it is admittedly not constantly enjoyed, the "power
to withdraw ourselves from the changes of time into
our innermost self" is not at every moment exercised.

This general conception of the eternal yet all-
embracing moment, as well as other aspects of the
complex of ideas which we have already observed,
finds its most eloquent American echo in Emerson's
"The Over-Soul":

> We live in succession, in division, in parts, in par-
> ticles. Meantime *within* man is the soul of the
> whole; the wise silence; the universal beauty to
> which every part and particle is equally related;
> the eternal *One*. And this deep power in which we
> exist and whose beatitude is all accessible to us, is
> not only all-sufficing and perfect in every hour, but
> the act of seeing and the thing seen, the seer and
> the spectacle, the subject and the object, are one.
> We see the world piece by piece, as the sun, the
> moon, the animal, the tree; but the whole of which
> these are the shining parts is the Soul. . . . All goes

to show that the soul in man . . . is not a function,
like the power of memory, of calculation, of comparison, but uses these as hands and feet; . . . is
not the intellect or the will, but the master of the
intellect and the will; is the background of our
being, in which they lie—an immensity not possessed and that cannot be possessed. . . . The Soul
. . . abolishes time and space. The influence of the
senses has in most men overpowered the mind to
that degree that the walls of time and space have
come to look real and insurmountable. . . . Yet
space and time are but inverse measures of the
force of the Soul. The spirit sports with time,—
  "Can crowd eternity into an hour,
  Or stretch an hour to eternity."[16]

That Bergson's intuition of *le moi profond* is conceived by him as a way of transcending time, in the
ordinary sense of the word, is evident. He calls it, to
be sure, the experience of "real duration"; but this
is a duration not subject to the intellect's categories of
quantity and number. It is "intensity" without extension; it is "indivisible though moving"; it is a "succession without distinction," a "solidarity"; its elements "interpenetrate" and have not *la moindre ten-
dance à s'extérioriser les uns par rapport aux autres.*[17]
"Considered in themselves, the deep-seated conscious

[16] "The Over-Soul," *Essays* (1st ser., 1903), p. 269. Much
even of the phrasing is reminiscent of Schelling's *Von der
Weltseele.*

[17] *Time and Free Will* (London, 1910), p. 137.

states . . . intermingle in such a way that we cannot tell whether they are one or several, nor even examine them from this point of view without at once altering their nature." In his *Introduction to Metaphysics* Bergson observes that there are different grades of the apprehension of duration, in some of which the fusion of moments is closer and more comprehensive than in others. As we ascend this series, "we approach a duration which *strains*, contracts, and intensifies itself more and more; at the limit would be eternity; not a conceptual eternity, which is an eternity of death, but an eternity of life—a living and therefore still moving eternity in which one's own particular duration would be included: an eternity which would be the concentration of all duration, as materiality is its dispersion." Even the idea of a certain *order* of succession in time, we are told, "involves the idea of space, and should not be used in the definition of time." "A sufficiently powerful act of attention and one sufficiently detached from practical interests, would . . . embrace the entire past history of the conscious person"—though Bergson, it must be noted, apparently does not find it including the future history. Thus his *durée réelle* might, with the change of a single word, be described in the terms of Boethius's famous definition of eternity: *vitae praeteritae tota simul ac perfecta possessio*. It is through the reading of the attributes of space into those of time that this indivisible present, for our ordinary experience, gets broken up into mutually external moments. Space and spatialized time are necessary for the life of action— that is, for the activity of the body, which is the instrument of action. Our ordinary perception and our ordinary and fragmentary memory—in which also past time is apprehended as mutually exclusive moments of experience—provide, as it were, the field in which, and the intellectual tool through which, the body can act effectively in a material world. But, as we have seen, the material world is not the true reality revealed in intuition, and the life of action is not the road to metaphysical knowledge. "When we pass from pure perception to memory, we definitely abandon matter for spirit"; "pure spirit" *is* "pure memory"; and "on the plane of pure memory . . . our mind retains in all its details the picture of our past life." This is approximated when, renouncing "the interests of effective action, we replace ourselves in the life of dream"; for "in certain dreams and somnambulistic states," and "in cases of sudden suffocation in men drowned or hanged," memories "which we believed abolished reappear with striking completeness."[18]

[18] *Matter and Memory* (Eng. tr.), pp. 313, 322, 199, 200 and *passim*. The similarity to the ideas of Coleridge outlined above is obvious.

Here, then, we seem to have once more, in a different terminology, the same notion of an experience of the Self in an indivisible present moment, wherein, none the less, all that is contained in the other moments, at least of "the time that has run its course," is in some manner immediately included. And upon the strange charm and the vitalizing potency of this experience Bergson, in his discourse on *L'intuition philosophique*, dilates in language interestingly similar to that of a passage of Schelling's already quoted.[19]

When we bring back our perception to its source, we shall have a knowledge of a new kind without needing to have recourse to new faculties. . . . Let us but resume possession of ourselves as we really are, in a present moment, rich and elastic in content, which we can dilate infinitely towards the past by removing the screen which hides us from ourselves; let us but grasp the external world as *it* is— not merely its surface, the present, but its depth, the immediate past which presses upon and gives its impulsion to the present; let us, in a word, but habituate ourselves to see all things *sub specie durationis:*—and then what was rigid in our galvanized perception becomes relaxed, what was sleeping wakes, what was dead becomes alive. The satisfaction which art can give only to those favored by nature and by fortune, and to them only at rare intervals, such satisfactions philosophy, so under-

[19] P. 78 above.

stood, will furnish to all of us, at every moment, by
breathing the breath of life into the phantoms which
surround us, and by revivifying ourselves.[20]

Certainly, the reader of these words, and of the
corresponding passage in Schelling, cannot but assume
that these utterances, strange and perplexing as they
may sound, are attempts to report a kind of actual
experience which these philosophers have had, and
believe, therefore, that others may have; and, indeed,
the claim to an essentially empirical basis which we
have seen to be characteristic of this type of philosophy, implies that they are speaking of what they
have directly experienced. Though both Schelling and
Bergson defend their doctrines of the indivisibility of
time in the deeper self by reasoning, it would be inconsistent with their principles to admit that it can be
discovered or conclusively verified by reasoning. We
must therefore attempt to determine, if possible, what
is the specific nature of this state of consciousness—
this "psychological eternity," in Aldous Huxley's
phrase—of which those who profess to have enjoyed
it usually write more rhapsodically than clearly—or
at the least, to find analogues or approximations to it
in experiences with which we are acquainted—and
also, if we can, to make out what they find in it to
evoke such rhapsodies.

[20] *Op. cit.*

Sometimes it appears to be identified by Bergson with what may be called the limiting instance of memory—instantaneous total recall of the individual's past experience. But other things said of it are difficult to reconcile with this interpretation. For the actual experiences in which such recall is said to be exemplified, or at any rate approximated, are *not* open to us "at every moment," but are admittedly conditioned by exceptional—and often by no means agreeable—physical states; the only specific examples of its possibility that are mentioned are "cases of sudden suffocation in men drowned or hanged," "feverish states," and certain (unspecified) types of dream and somnambulism. These, surely, can hardly be the gates to that initiation into the ultimate mystery of Being of which Bergson, like Schelling, writes so fervently. Supposing—what I take to be questionable in fact—that drowning men see all their past lives in a single moment, I doubt whether they find it so voluptuous an experience as these philosophers describe; and in any case, a philosopher who never had himself been drowned or hanged is not in a position to testify that it is so, from his own experience. It is observable, in fact, that, when they seem to identify their "intellectual" or "metaphysical intuition" with total recall, none of these philosophers assure us that they have themselves known such recall; they refer us, for the evidence of it, to what is reported by or of other men. We have, in truth, no reason whatever for believing that either Bergson or anyone else has ever, even momentarily, been blest, or curst, with so remarkably good a memory. And even if there could be shown to be instances of correct, complete, and simultaneous remembrance, they would not satisfy the requirements of the description of the metaphysical intuition. For it is not our past experience in their own identity as acts or events that become present together in memory. What is present is a set of images or verbal symbols of them, and it is of the essence of the memory-experience that the events themselves are apprehended as having been "mutually external" and, with respect to their original or real existence, as external to the moment in which they are remembered. Upon this fact, indeed, Bergson himself on occasion insists. Past time *is* divided; *nous divisons le déroulé, mais non pas le déroulement.* "Time is not a line over which we can pass again. Certainly, *once it has passed*, we are justified in picturing the successive moments as external to one another and in thus thinking of a line traversing space; but it must be understood that this line does not symbolize the time which is passing, but the time which is past."[21] How, then, can it be said that, at the instant of remembrance, what

[21] *Durée et simultanéité*, p. 63; italics mine.

is presented for awareness is an indivisible unity, without "numerical multiplicity"? Memory, in which the mind is preoccupied with the past, and therefore with the thought of "moments external to one another," should, for Bergson, be the worst possible example of the experience of "real duration."

We must, therefore, look further for the nature of the experience which may be supposed to lie behind the sort of language that we have found Bergson using about the time-transcending intuition. And there is in fact another mode of awareness to which Bergson, still following Schelling, quite explicitly points for the exemplification of "pure time" or "real duration"—*i.e.*, of psychological eternity. Both find it in a feature of musical experience. In his essay *On the Relation of the Real and the Ideal in Nature*,[22] Schelling attempts—in a manner a little different from that previously cited—what Coleridge called "the extrication of the notions of space and time." Each of these is the "negation" of the essential attribute of the other. That of space is simultaneity and the mutual externality of its parts. "Time, on the contrary, takes away (*aufhebt*) mutual externality (*das Auseinander*) and posits the inner identity of things. But while thus negating the nullity (*das Nicht-*

[22] Prefixed to *Von der Weltseele*, 1798; 2d ed., 1806; 3d ed., 1809.

*ige*) of space, it introduces a nullity of its own, namely, the successiveness in things, *das Nacheinander in den Dingen*." But there is a "principle" (we need not here inquire just what it is) which "penetrates through time, . . . foresees the future, brings the present into accord with the past, and completely takes away that loose connection with one another which things have in time," *i.e.*, in succession (*jene lose Verknüpfung der Dinge in der Zeit*). And we can, says Schelling, find instances of this in particular phenomena; such is "a Klang [probably in the sense of the sound of bells], which, though it belongs to time, nevertheless, because it is as it were organized *in* time, is a true totality," and exemplifies how "time, *as* time, is negated."[23] Just how a single tone does so is not, indeed, made very clear; a musical phrase would seem an example more to Schelling's purpose. But we may with some probability gather what he had in mind from another writer. When Jean Paul, in his *Vorschule der Aesthetik* (1804, 1812) sought to define "the essence of the Romantic" he observed that music is a more "romantic" art than painting for the significant reason that in the former alone can there be a sort of fusion and interpenetration of the ele-

---

[23] *SW*, 1, II, 368–70. All this is interwoven with obscure notions, belonging to the Schellingian *Naturphilosophie*, about light and gravity, which are not pertinent to the present point.

ments of a temporal sequence; and, by the same criterion, he found some musical instruments to be more "romantic" than others.

> No color is so romantic as a tone; for . . . a tone is never heard singly, but *is always threefold, fusing the past and the future with the present, just as Romanticism does.* Thus it is that the bell, among percussion instruments, evokes best the romantic spirit, because its tones live longest and die away most slowly. Next to it comes, among stroked instruments, the musical-glasses (*harmonica*), and next, among wind instruments, the French horn (*Waldhorn*) and the organ.[24]

These, however, are but arrows, pointing, indeed, to the sort of experience *in* time which is supposed to transcend the divisions *of* time, but not greatly illuminating it. Bergson has made a much more serious effort than (so far as I know or recall) any of his German precursors to elucidate the matter psychologically— one is tempted to say, to analyze introspectively the feature of musical experience in which he finds the nature of the indivisible *durée réelle* primarily and best exhibited. The results of this effort are intimated in some passages of his published writings, but perhaps even better in an unpublished letter. In reply to some criticisms of his doctrine concerning time

[24] *Jean Pauls Werke* (1841 ed.), IX, 355; italics mine.

which I had expressed—chiefly on the ground that it is self-contradictory—he was good enough, many years ago, to write me explaining more fully the empirical source and grounds of that doctrine, and also dealing directly with the charge of self-contradiction. Since, however, this explanation, together with the comments upon it which it seems to me worth while to offer, would make too long a digression from the primarily historical themes of these lectures, it is printed as an appendix.

# Lecture IV

We are now to witness a series of transformation scenes or dissolving views, in which certain of the conceptions we have thus far been observing surprisingly present themselves in shapes quite different from those which they at first wore— and sometimes turn into their own opposites. It is not in all cases that our philosophers deliberately changed their doctrines, explicitly abandoned the theses which we have found them expressing (though eventually that happened in some instances); it is that what were nominally the same theses took on meanings distinct from and often incongruous with those which, in the order of our exposition, we have hitherto seen attaching to them. It is still with revelations declared to be accessible only through a faculty of knowledge superior to the "understanding" that we shall be concerned, in what just now follows; but these further revelations seem (at least to the Understanding) hard to reconcile with those which have so far been reported.

The "reality" of which we are, through the "Rea-

101

son" or the "intellectual intuition," made immediately aware is, as we have seen, according to the philosophies which we have been considering, the Ego —the "true self," exempt from the divisions and limitations of time. But how many such time-transcending Egos are there? A kind of entity designated by the first personal pronoun might naturally be supposed to exist in as many instances as there are conscious individuals who can say "This is I." The eternal selves, it might appear, should be as numerous as the empirical persons engaged in their various temporal concerns—so that you might find from the catalogue of a college how many noumenal Egos have their sensible manifestations there. The language of these philosophers often seems plainly to refer to a plurality of such Egos, and I have hitherto been speaking as if there might be many of them. For Kant there were. If *his* noumenal Egos had not been as numerous as human persons, in the ordinary sense, they would not have performed the function which is, in the motivation of this part of his philosophy, their *raison d'être*. For that function was to bear the moral responsibility for the deeds of individuals—and especially, to take the blame for their misdeeds.[1] But what concerns us at this point is that Schelling already in the earliest

[1] Kant's arguments for this thesis will be examined in the following lecture.

phase of his philosophizing, unlike Kant, saw that, if
the category of number is a product of the Understanding, it cannot be applicable to the "real," that is, the
noumenal self. *Das Ich,* in short, is not only distinct
from the empirical personality of the individual, but
is incapable of plurality; you cannot without contradiction speak of this, that or the other Ego. It is *gar
nicht durch Zahl bestimmbar.* It is not merely that
there *is* only one existent example of the kind of being
that the pure Ego is, but that its essence implies uniqueness. Ordinarily, says Schelling, "when numerical
uniqueness is asserted of anything, the concept of a
*class* is presupposed, of which the thing is conceived
as the only actual member, but with the implication
of the (real and logical) *possibility* that it might not
be the only one; *i.e.,* it is the one only in respect of
its existence, not of its essence. Only the Ego is *absolutely* one, [since] it cannot be subsumed under any
class concept. . . . For a concept (*Begriff*) is something which *combines* a multiplicity into a unity; the
Ego, therefore, cannot be a concept, . . . for it neither
combines nor is combined, but is *absolute* unity. It is
therefore neither a genus nor a species nor an individual, since these notions are thinkable only through
a reference to plurality (*Vielheit*). One who can take
the Ego for a concept, or assert of it *either* numerical
oneness or numerical multiplicity, knows nothing of

the Ego."[2] This might seem to imply that we cannot think or talk about the Ego at all, since we cannot conceive of an entity that is neither a genus nor a species nor yet an individual—neither many nor one. But Schelling manifestly did think about the Ego, and proceeded to talk a great deal about it; and what his argument here comes to is merely a denial that it is an individual in the usual sense; namely, an individual *member* of a possible genus. It is an individual in the absolute sense that there could not conceivably be a *class* of existents of the same kind. The essential point is, then, that there cannot be many Egos, but only one.

It is, moreover, an Ego devoid of all the particular attributes and relations which belong to the concrete objects of which the Understanding conceives. Since the category of number is strictly inapplicable to it, it can no more possess a plurality of attributes than a plurality of embodiments or instances. Even the apparent duality of subject and object, from which the problem of knowledge takes its rise, is in the Ego, as we have seen, resolved into identity. It is in the most absolute sense indivisible. There is only one positive statement that you can make about it: that it has—or rather, that it is—Being: "It primal form

[2] *Vom Ich als Prinzip der Philosophie* (1795), SW, 1, I, 183–84.

is that of pure being . . . and pure being is thinkable
only in the Ego" (*seine Urform ist die des reinen
Seins, . . . und reines Sein ist nur im Ich Denkbar*).[3]
The reason why, for Schelling, "pure Being is thinkable only in the Ego" is apparently to be found in
those reasonings about "immediacy" which have
been set forth in the second lecture; nothing can be
immediately, and therefore certainly, known to exist
except the knowing self. It does not, in fact, follow
from the proposition that nothing but the Self can be
indubitably *known* to exist (even if this be admitted),
that nothing else *can* exist, or that "the Self" *means*
just "Being," and nothing else. But Schelling seems
to have passed from the first proposition to the second
and third without being conscious of a logically illicit
transition. When the transition is made, the Ego proves
—though Schelling himself would not have liked so to
describe it—to be the ultimate abstraction, the notion
to which, because it is prior to all other notions, none
of the others are applicable; it could be defined in
the same terms as Spinoza's "substance," as that
which *in se est et per se concipitur* and has "need of
the concept of no other thing in order that it may be
conceived"—or rather, as Schelling would express it,
in order that it may be intuited. Schelling, indeed, observes that Spinoza's philosophy, "in what is true and

[3] *Ibid.*, pp. 221, 223.

fundamental in it, is an expression of the *intellektuelle Anschauung*."[4] In strictness of speech, Schelling goes on to observe in the *System des transcendentalen Idealismus* (1800), we cannot even use "existence" as a *predicate* of the Ego. "Since the Ego possesses none of the predicates which belong to things, the paradox that one cannot say of the Ego that it *is* becomes intelligible. One cannot say that the Ego is, simply because it is itself *Being*. The eternal, time-transcending act of self-consciousness which we call the Ego is that which gives existence to all things, and therefore does not need any other 'being' to support it."[5] Anything *is* only by virtue of possessing reality (*Realität*). Its essence (*essentia, Wesen*) is reality, because it owes its *esse* solely to the infinite reality; it *is* only in so far as the primal source (*Urquelle*) of reality imparts reality to it. "The Ego, therefore, is not only the cause of the existence but also of the essence of all that is." Speaking in a figure, one may say: "The absolute Ego describes an infinite sphere, which com-

---

[4] *Ibid.*, p. 194. "Spinoza recognized that, prior to all existence, a pure, immutable *Ursein*, a self-subsistent something, must underlie all coming into being and passing-away; and that first in and through this, all that has existence attains unity of existence (*die Einheit des Daseins*). Only, Spinoza did not see that this *Urform alles Seins* must be conceived as the Ego."

[5] *SW*, 1, III, 376.

prehends all reality."[6] "On my Ego is based all existence; my Ego is everything, in it and for it is
everything that is: I take away my Ego and everything
that is, is nothing. (*Auf meinem Ich ruht alles Dasein:
mein Ich ist alles, in ihm und zu ihm ist alles, was
ist; ich nehme mein Ich hinweg, und alles was ist,
ist nichts.*)[7] If this were said of the individual self—
as the words "*mein Ich*" suggest—it would, obviously,
be evidence of a delusion of grandeur—Professor
Schelling's Ego so inflated that he imagines himself
to be the universe. But it is, as we have just been
seeing, not Professor Schelling's Ego that is in question; it is the single universal Ego which can no more
be ascribed to any one finite individual than to another.

In a writing a little later than that from which I
have last been quoting—the *Exposition of My System
of Philosophy*, 1801—Schelling dilates at length upon
the conception of the fundamental, or "true," reality
as "absolute identity." He here prefers to call it "the
absolute Reason," perhaps because he wished not to
have it confused with the private or multiple Egos;
but the terms in which he characterizes it are the same
as those applied to the intuited Self in the treatise
*On the Ego as the Principle of Philosophy*. The knowl-

[6] *Op. cit.*, pp. 195, 191.
[7] *Ibid.*, p. 193.

edge of it is "the only unconditional knowledge,"
since "Being belongs to its essence," and not to the
essence of anything else; it is "the total *indifference*,"
or indistinguishable unity, "of subject and object,"
and, one may say, of all predicates, since in it, as
*reine Identität*, "nothing can be distinguished,"
or differentiated, *Nichts unterscheidbar sei*—or, as
Hegel was satirically to describe it, it is "the night
in which all cows are black." This *Identitätssystem*
has usually been described as a new phase in Schelling's philosophizing, a departure from his earlier
principles; yet he himself, I think, never so regarded
it, and it was, in fact, implicit, if not always explicit,
in his doctrine from the first, as he himself declared.

Thus, in spite of its name, the entity which had
been declared to be the immediately apprehensible
core of the existence of every man now presents historically familiar features—or more precisely, a
historically familiar absence of features. Whether
called the Ego or the Reason, it seems not distinguishable from the "Being" of Parmenides, the "super-
essentially superexisting One" of Neoplatonism, the
Âtman of the Vedântist monism (with which, indeed,
Schopenhauer soon identified it), the God of Scholastic theology, when Scholastic theology followed the
*via negativa*, which was for it admittedly the truer
way of thinking of the divine nature. The summary

exposition given of the essence of the Catholic conception of God by one of the best qualified living interpreters of the Thomistic doctrine, Professor Gilson, is, even in its phraseology, almost identical with Schelling's exposition of the nature of the Ego—except that the one starts with an act of faith, the other, ostensibly, with an act of self-intuition. I quote briefly, to enable you to observe the parallel, from Mr. Gilson's Gifford Lectures on *The Spirit of Medieval Philosophy*.

> When God [in the Book of Exodus] says that He is being, . . . *Ego sum qui sum*—it can only mean this: that He is the pure act of existing. . . . It is not as a concept that God would have us think of him nor even as a being whose content would be that of a concept. Beyond all sensible images, *and all conceptual determinations,* God affirms himself as the absolute act of being in its pure actuality. Our *concept* of God, a mere feeble analogue of a reality which overflows it in every direction, can be made explicit only in the judgment: Being is Being, an absolute positing of that which, lying beyond every object, contains in itself the sufficient reason of objects.[8]

Where the Catholic metaphysician calls this pure and primal Being by the name of God—and thereby evokes a whole complex of associated religious ideas

[8] *Op. cit.,* pp. 51–53.

and their concomitant emotional attitudes—Schelling calls it the inner Self.

> Since the Ego in itself is absolute identity through its mere existence, it makes no difference whether the highest principle be expressed as 'I am I': or as 'I am.' "
>
> (Da das Ich seinem selbst nach, durch sein blosses Sein, als absolute Identität gesetzt ist, so ist es gleichviel, ob der oberste Grundsatz so ausgedrückt wird: *Ich bin ich; oder: Ich bin*)[9]

But since the *nature* of that which the two philosophers are, in these passages, talking about is the same nature, it does not appear to make any difference in strict logic whether it is called "God" or *das Ich*.

Yet, though the attributes—or absence of attributes —of the Ego were essentially the same as those of the negative Absolute of the radically otherworldly theology of all ages, the difference of name was far from unimportant. For when this pure unmultiplied and unmultipliable Being was called the Self of the individual, it could, in the first place, be more easily conceived as capable of being directly intuited *by* the individual, and therefore of being known with the intimacy, certainty, and assurance that attach to immediacy. Religion, Schelling observes, has commonly conceived of God as an "object" over against the Self;

[9] *Vom Ich* . . . , SW, 1, I, 179.

but "in so far as he is [in this sense] an object, he falls outside the sphere of *our* knowledge, and therefore cannot be *for us* the ultimate point on which the whole of this sphere depends. We wish to know not what God is for himself, but what he is for us, in relation to our knowledge (*Wissen*); God may, indeed, be for himself completely the ground (*Realgrund*) of his own knowledge but this he is not for us, because he is himself for us an object, and therefore in the chain of our knowledge presupposes *another* ground to lend him necessity [of being] for this knowledge."[10] In other words, if conceived as an external reality, God cannot be immediately, and therefore cannot be certainly, known. But the Self—however fully invested with the metaphysical attributes of deity—is in no sense an Other, which we must by some means attain unto; it is, by hypothesis, what we already fundamentally and unalterably *are*, and what we can discover ourselves to be if we will turn away from the world of sense and time and material things and simply resume possession of our own being.

Moreover, the use of the first personal pronoun for this supersensible and time-transcending entity potentially gave to the thought of it a different poetic and emotional value, lent it a new sort of metaphysical pathos. For the first personal pronoun, after all, when

[10] *Ibid.*, p. 165.

used by John and James and William and Henry, carries with it for each of them an ineradicable connotation of proprietorship, as the substantive "God," or the metaphysical abstraction "the Absolute," does not. It is one thing to say that God is an infinite and eternal and incorporeal being above all the vicissitudes of time, superior to the realm of sense; it is, in its emotional effect, quite a different thing to say that "I" am such a being. When you say *that*—even though you should, with Schelling, add, as a metaphysical theorem, that there is not a plurality of "I's"—you can hardly avoid feeling a certain aggrandizement of your own personality, or a heightening of the dignity of man in general. And it was this psychological consequence of the *terminology* of Schelling and his disciples that (I suspect) gave to their characterizations of the intuition of the Ego much of their appeal and of their moral effect. They provided a means—and a means supposed to be justified by a profound metaphysical insight—whereby a man could think highly of himself—not, indeed, of his everyday, pedestrian self, immersed in vulgar tasks and petty ambitions, but of his true Self, which is raised above all these things and dwells in a nobler realm of being. And finally, it was easy, especially for poets and for popularizers of these conceptions, simply to forget that, according to the Schellingian reasoning, there

cannot be many "I's," and to take the first personal
pronoun literally; and not less easy to take it in both
ways in turn, as one's mood or the exigencies of one's
argument required: now as the deeper essence of the
individual person, now as an indivisible unity under-
lying all separate persons and therefore constituting
a species of mystical communion between them.

In this last turn of thought there was an illicit
transition from one conception to another and inconsistent one. If "being" belongs only to the one indivisible Ego it would seem to follow that "being" (in
the sense of actual existence) cannot be asserted of
anything else—that separate persons and all the seeming multiplicity of the objects of experience are not
merely phenomena but illusions. It was this conclusion that Schopenhauer drew from the metaphysical premise which he shared with Schelling's *Identitätssystem*. The conclusion was itself, it is true, a
self-contradictory one; for you do not annul the plurality of experiences and of things experienced by calling
them "illusions." In the very act of denying them
you admit that they in some sense *are;* an illusion
to which all mankind is admittedly subject and which
the philosopher exhorts you to overcome is obviously
there to *be* overcome, and is no pure nonentity. But
to Schopenhauer, as to Shankara and the sages of the
Upanishads before him, it seemed to be meaningful

and important to call all the choir of heaven and furniture of earth simply "Nothing." And Schelling too at times speaks in a fashion indistinguishable from the Vedântist acosmism. "The nothingness of things," he declares, is "not a mere nothingness with respect to quality, but a nothingness with respect to existence, *ein Nichts der Existenz nach;* and it can in no wise be regarded as antithetic to the All or the Absolute, since it has no existence antithetic to it [i.e., to the absolute], but simply no existence at all."[11]

But few Western philosophers have been satisfied with a flight from the Many to the One unless they could fly back again, bringing with them, so to say, some speculative or practical gains applicable in the world of plurality and becoming. Of Schelling, at all events, this is conspicuously true. Having, in the Parmenidean manner, asserted, in the most unqualified terms, the sole "reality" of pure, absolute, indivisible Being, he proceeds to fetch back the Immutable One *into* the realm of the mutable Many, yet (supposedly) without loss of the proper character of either, without denial of the perfect unity and eternality of the One nor of the real multiplicity and

[11] *Aphorismen zur Einleitung in die Naturphilosophie* (1806), *SW*, 1, VII, 194.

temporality of the Many. His object, he tells us in his *Von der Weltseele* (1798), is to show how necessary this conception of the pure unity of Being, the indivisible and unchangeable One, is even for natural science. The *Naturforscher*, in studying the changing phenomena of the inorganic and organic world, is brought to recognize as "the primary cause of all these changes and the ultimate ground of all nature's activity" something which "because it is present everywhere, is nowhere, and because it is all, can be nothing specific or determinate; for which, therefore, language has no proper designation; and the idea of which the most ancient philosophy (to which our own, after fetching a compass, is now returning) has handed down to us only in poetic images."[12] The treatise *On the World-Soul* is consequently, in spite of its title, chiefly an attempt at a "philosophical" science of nature, and deals with such subjects as gravitation, light and heat, electricity, and the origin and processes of plant and animal life.

With these weird parts of Schelling's *Natur-philosophie*, however, we are (fortunately) not here concerned. What is pertinent to the present theme is that the reality revealed in intuition now appears in what would seem a still different guise from any

[12] *Von der Weltseele, Vorrede zur Ersten Auflage, SW*, I, II, 348.

of those which we have hitherto been observing. What was first introduced as the immediately experienced inner self of each of us, and then as the unmultipliable unity of "pure Being," without parts or positive attributes, now presents itself as yet another historically familiar entity—the *anima mundi*. The conception of this kind of entity, though it has appeared in more than one form, has usually been a device resorted to by metaphysicians who, having identified "true reality" with a being "one" in the strictest sense —timeless, indivisible, suprasensible, extra-mundane —have nevertheless felt a need of connecting this transcendent, and (for our thought) negative, Absolute with the world of sense and diversity and change. When the notion of the Cosmic Soul first clearly presents itself in Western thought, in Plato's *Timaeus,* it is expressly as a means of "overcoming" the antithesis of "the indivisible existence that is ever in the same state and the divisible existence that undergoes becoming in bodies." To accomplish this the Demiurge created "a third form of existence compounded of both"; and "taking the three, he blended them all together into one form (ἰδέα), by forcing Otherness into union with Sameness, hard though they are to mix. And when, mingling them with Existence, he had made of them one out of three, he forthwith distributed this whole into as many parts as

was fitting; and each part was a mixture of Sameness
and of Otherness and of Being."[13] Thus, by this
strange metaphysical fusion of opposites, each part,
each particular thing in the world, though "other"
than all its fellow-members of the realm of "divisible
existence," was also the "same" with them; for the
Soul was present *without* division, and therefore completely, in each, and was also (as the older traditional
conception of the soul connoted) the animating principle, the "life" of each. Such, at least, was the fully
developed conception of the *anima mundi* as it appears in Neoplatonism. Thus Plotinus writes:

> Even as the bright beams of the sun enlighten a dark
> cloud and give it a golden border, so the soul when
> it enters into the body of the heaven gives it life
> and immortality and awakens it from sleep. . . .
> The soul gives itself to every point in this vast body,
> but itself is not divided; it does not split itself up in
> order to give life to each individual. All things
> live by the soul in its entirety; it is all present every-
> where, like the Father who begat it, both in its
> unity and its universality.[14]

This conception, then, was taken over by numerous
philosophers and poets of the period, 1780-1830. It
was certainly no innovation, and hardly a revival, on

[13] *Timaeus*, 35a, b.
[14] *Enneads*, V, 1, 2.

their part; for it had been expressed in one of the most famous passages of the most widely read philosophical poem of the eighteenth century. There are few more curious examples in literature of the combination of close similarity, or virtual identity, of conceptual content with extreme difference in poetic style and even emotional tone, than that to be observed when one compares a passage in Wordsworth's *Tintern Abbey* poem with the lines of Pope near the end of the first Epistle of the *Essay on Man:*

> All are but parts of one stupendous whole,
> Whose body Nature is, and God the soul;
> That, chang'd thro' all, and yet in all the same,
> Great in the earth as in th'ethereal frame,
> Warms in the sun, refreshes in the breeze,
> Glows in the stars, and blossoms in the trees,
> Lives thro' all life, extends thro' all extent,
> Spreads undivided, operates unspent;
> Breathes in our soul, informs our mortal part,
> As full, as perfect, in a hair as heart;
> As full, as perfect, in vile man that mourns,
> As the rapt Seraph that adores and burns;
> To him no high, no low, no great, no small;
> He fills, he bounds, connects and equals all.

Pope, I fear, had never knowingly experienced the *intellektuelle Anschauung* and he knew nothing of the distinction of the Reason and the Understanding; he nevertheless had expressed concisely but precisely the principal implications of that conception of the indivisible One as also the *Weltseele*, which, by Schelling and the contemporaries whom he influenced, was supposed to have been attained only through the discovery of a new, or rediscovery of an old, way of knowing. For Schelling liked to dwell especially upon the thought of the One as "connecting" and "filling" all things. It is the bond of union between the parts of nature, and—being everywhere because it is nowhere, that is, nowhere in particular—it is intimately interfused in all of them. He now adopts the traditional language of religion; the being which thus links together and pervades the Many, though sometimes still called the Reason, is usually named God:

> The goal of the most sublime science can be nothing but this: to make manifest the true reality—reality in the strictest sense, the presence, the living *being—being-there (das lebendige Da-sein)*, of a God in the whole of things and in each individual thing. . . . God is the One in the totality of things; this One is recognizable in every part of matter, all lives in it. But equally immediately present and recognizable in every part is the All in the One as it everywhere opens up life, and even in the transitory unfolds the flower of eternity. The sacred bond through which the two are one we ourselves experience in our own life and its alternations. . . . That which links all things together *(das All-Kopula)*

exists in ourselves as the Reason, and bears witness to our spirit. It is no longer here a question of anything supernatural or extra-natural, but of that which is immediately near, of that which alone is real, to which we belong and in which we are . . . [For] this science which we teach and clearly know, "immanence" and "transcendence" are completely and equally empty words; for it annuls this antithesis, and in it everything flows together into one god-filled world *(alles zusammenfliesst zu Einer Gotterfüllten Welt).*[15]

The language which the poets and Schelling use in speaking of this World-Soul is dithyrambic, and sounds self-contradictory; but it could be construed as expressing (or, rather, concealing) a conception which is by no means unintelligible or paradoxical. The seemingly remarkable properties ascribed in these passages to "God" as the *anima mundi* are, in fact, simply the properties of any general idea of a quality or attribute. Consider, for example, the concept of the pure *quality* redness, and its relation to any particular red patches occupying several determinate spatial regions. There is, by hypothesis, redness in each of these regions. But you cannot say that a *part* of redness in general is in one of the regions and other parts in other regions. For redness, in so far as it is conceived purely as a quality, has no parts. Nobody,

[15] *Von der Weltseele, SW,* I, II, 376–77.

presumably, supposes that there is a certain divisible
quantity of redness laid up in a sort of Platonic
heaven, a portion of which must be chipped off to
produce a red patch here, another portion to produce
another red patch there, and so on, so that in the end
all the redness there is might conceivably be used up,
to provide a sufficient number of patches. Redness, *as*
a quality, is as completely present in one patch as in
another; it is, in fact, totally present or—as Professor
Whitehead would say—"ingredient" in each of them.
It is "as full, as perfect, in a (red) hair as [in a]
(red) heart." (I quote with reluctance so atrocious a
line.) And the same is true of the general attribute
"Being," so long as it is strictly conceived *as* an attribute expressed by what the grammarians call an
abstract noun. If you admit that it means something
to say that anything that exists has "being," then,
wherever something exists, "being" is present—not
a part of it, but the whole of it, for it no more has
parts than redness has. If, then, you conceive of "God"
or "the Soul," not concretely as an individual, but
as "pure Being"—the *property* of "being" as such—
there is no paradox in saying that it is equally and
completely present in everything that is; such a statement would be simply a harmless truism. But the
terms "God," or the "universal Soul," do *not* usually
convey the conception of a general quality or attribute,

but of a concrete entity, an individual; and of an individual—supposing it to be one capable of having spatial location at all—it *is* paradoxical and self-contradictory to say that it is completely present in one place and also completely present in another place at the same time—or at all times. When these considerations are borne in mind, it is possible to see why the language of the metaphysicians and the poets about God as the "soul of the world" sounds so mystifying, and also how, to those who used it, it nevertheless, through a confusion of ideas, could seem meaningful and plausible. The confusion, I am suggesting, consisted in slipping over unconsciously from the notion of God as "pure Being"—*i.e.*, as that attribute or status which belongs, and belongs equally, to all "beings"—to the notion of *a* being—God as a unique, concrete existent—in short, in talking of a universal as if it were a particular.

But when this transition (whatever its explanation) took place, the world of particulars, of individual selves and of the objects of their experience, could no longer be regarded as mere illusion. If the World-Soul, however indivisible in itself, is also *present* in innumerable separate entities, if it "gives them life" and "connects them" with one another, then they cannot be—what we have previously been told by Schelling that they are—simply "nothing"; for to say that the Soul animates nothing and connects nothing is to say that it is *not* an animating or connecting power. Thus the acosmism to which we found Schelling brought by his "intellectual intuition" of the Ego is now—implicitly, if not always explicitly—abandoned. The oneness now predicated of "the Self" is not the kind of oneness that excludes multiplicity; on the contrary, it is the kind of oneness that presupposes and requires multiplicity. Not only are there, after all, many selves; there are also many sensible and temporal objects which are not, for any individual experiencer of them, describable as simply the unmultipliable Absolute Self. External nature, in short, after having first been reduced to the status of mere phenomenon, and then still further reduced (ostensibly) to sheer nonentity, is here—as a corollary of the transformation of the Ego into the *Weltseele*—restored, albeit somewhat equivocally, to the metaphysical dignity of "real" existence, a dignity the more impressive because "nature and the language of the sense" now apprehended as the manifestation of a mysterious and supersensible and ubiquitous presence—of (in Wordsworth's phrasing)

. . . Something far more deeply interfused,
Whose dwelling is the light of setting suns,
And the round ocean, and the living air,
And the blue sky, and in the mind of man:

A motion and a spirit that impels
All thinking things, all objects of all thought,
And rolls through all things.

The entity which Wordsworth speaks of in these terms —indivisibly and identically present in all natural objects and all human individuals, and giving activity and movement to them all—is the same as Pope was describing in the lines quoted from the *Essay on Man;* and both poets were, consciously or not, echoing the Plotinian conception of the World-Soul. But to Wordsworth this idea had an emotional value which it did not have for Pope. For the "Nature" of which the former was thinking was not really the miscellaneous aggregate of physical existences— "hairs" and "hearts" and stars, along with "seraphs" and whatever extraterrestrial entities there may be. It consisted solely of the objects that can be, and for Wordsworth were, the sources of intense feelings and aesthetic delight. The susceptibility to these feelings Wordsworth tells us that he had from childhood. But when there came to him the conception of these sensible appearances as also the "presence" of a universal and omnipotent though insensible being, "something far more deeply interfused," these feelings received for him a sort of higher sanction and a further emotional intensification: *"Therefore"*—he declares in the lines immediately following those quoted—

Therefore am I still
A lover of the meadows and the woods,
And mountains, and of all that mighty world
Of eye and ear.[16]

[16] For a full and careful examination of the evidence as to the place of the notion of the *anima mundi* among Wordsworth's rather heterogeneous store of quasi-metaphysical ideas, see Raymond D. Havens's *The Mind of a Poet* (1941), pp. 190–98.

# *Lecture V*

We are now to note in the doctrines of most of the writers thus far mentioned concerning the distinction between the Reason (or the intellectual intuition) and the Understanding—that is, between the true or "metaphysical" knowledge of "reality" and the specious though practically useful knowledge of "appearances" which constitutes natural science— another and, in the main, a quite different version of that distinction, not hitherto indicated. Before proceeding to the exposition of the second, let us recall the first in a very syncopated form.

We saw in the second lecture that the primary quest of the intuitionists was for an "immediate" knowledge, a direct apprehension, of that which is indubitably *existent;* that this (as they argued) cannot be given either through sense-perception or through concepts, or by reasoning about the logical relations or implications of concepts, but only by the Ego's consciousness of itself, in which the knower, the knowing act, and the reality known, subject and object, are identical; and that the reality thus revealed by the intuition of the inner Self is "ineffable," "repugnant to the very essence of language," since words are merely the symbols or counters which we employ to refer to sensible objects or to concepts. We also saw this immediately known inner Self of every conscious individual reduced (at least by Schelling and Schopenhauer) to one unmultipliable entity, and that One divested of all attributes or predicates except pure "Being"—the God of the negative theology— and then, by another turn of the kaleidoscope, presented as the "undivided," yet spatially and temporally ubiquitous World-Soul which imparts life and movement to "all thinking things, all objects of all thought." Through all this we noted that, in setting forth and defending their theses, these epistemologists actually made copious use of concepts and of logical (or would-be logical) reasonings about the implications of concepts, and did not really limit themselves to reporting the "immediate intuition of inwardly experienced facts"; but this, of course, was presumably an unintended and inadvertent deviation of these philosophers from their initial aim, and not a part of the doctrine they were propounding. That doctrine professed to banish concepts, and everything that could be "represented" by concepts, to the limbo of the "mere Understanding"—and thus to deny to them any claim to "reality."

But at this point some of our epistemologists—
and most patently of all, Schelling—forgot, or abandoned, the starting-point of their reasoning, as it has
been outlined in the preceding lectures. They found
themselves, after all, sure of certain truths about
"reality" which plainly can not be reconciled with
the proposition that a knower can not know "immediately," and thereby with certainty, anything except its
own act of knowing. That initial premise of the *Identitätssystem* obviously could by itself lead logically to
nothing more than solipsism—and the "solipsism of
the specious present." True, it did not in fact lead
Schelling to that barren outcome; he avoided it by that
succession of bold metamorphoses—they were actually
but not admittedly contradictions of his former premises—which we have seen him performing. But even
after these strange transmutations of the "Ego" had
been accomplished, Schelling and some other of these
philosophers discovered that they were equally and
"immediately" certain of several other theorems
which did not relate at all, or did not relate solely,
to their own "inner selves." These theorems, undeniably, contained general concepts; but they were concepts which, so to say, the "Understanding" could not
understand, and the theorems could not be proved by
reasoning; they were not deducible from, and in some
cases were (or seemed) contradictory of, the basic

assumptions of natural science in its "explanations" —its formulations of the causal processes which hold good of the physical world. Thus they were not within the province of the Understanding. Our apprehension of these concepts and our indubitable certainty of these theorems must, then, be due to the fact that the "higher" cognitive faculty, the Reason, enables us to intuit directly, to "see," realities, or properties of "reality," with which neither the ratiocinations of the intellect nor sense-perception, nor even the bare consciousness of our own existence, can make us acquainted.

I now turn to the exposition of some of these theorems.


## 1. *QUALITY* vs. *QUANTITY AND NUMBER*


It was one of the frequently reiterated theses of many so-called "Romantic" writers that the inferior cognitive—or rather, the pseudo-cognitive—faculty can think only in terms of quantities and numbers, that its operation is exemplified only in the mathematical sciences; and that, on the other hand, these categories are inapplicable to the realities which are known to us through the superior faculty, which apprehends only qualities. This doctrine, stated in the language of a species of faculty psychology—the usual antithesis of *Verstand* and *Vernunft*—is, of course, inconsistent with itself; for obviously the notion of number can and must be applied *to* qualities, if they are admitted to be many and distinguishable; color, *e.g.*, is a quality, and there are seven colors in the spectrum of the rainbow.

But it cannot be denied, I fear, that numerous philosophers of the period we are considering simply had a distaste—perhaps born of an inaptitude—for mathematics, and tended to "rationalize" this by, so to say, giving a low epistemological rating to that science, and consequently a low intellectual rating to those addicted to it. Let me recall to you a few examples of this.

Schopenhauer, in spite of elements in his philosophy which might have justified the opposite conclusion, wrote in *Die Welt als Wille und Vorstellung*[1] that "persons of genius" are characterized by "an aversion from mathematics," and that experience shows that "great geniuses in art never have any mathematical ability," while "eminent mathematicians have little susceptibility for the fine arts"—both of which, of course, were false generalizations. It is especially "the logical procedure of the mathematical

[1] Vol. I, sec. 36.

sciences" which, says Schopenhauer, "makes them repugnant to the genius," since this procedure gives no place to "genuine *insight*," but offers merely a chain of deductions. This rage against the mathematical found perhaps its most emotional expression in a passage by a French writer, Lamartine, who, speaking of the intellectual fashions of the period of the First Empire, "that incarnation of the materialistic philosophy of the eighteenth century," wrote:

> All those geometrizing men, who alone in those days held the public ear . . . fancied that they had forever dried up within us all the moral, the divine, the melodious elements of the human soul. . . . Everything was organized for the suppression of this resurrection of moral and poetic feeling; there was a general alliance of the mathematical studies against thought and poetry. *Number* (*le chiffre*) alone was permitted, honored, protected, rewarded. Ever since that time I have abhorred number, that negation of all thought; and there has remained the same feeling of horror for that jealous and exclusive power of mathematics, which the convict feels for the irons riveted upon his limbs. The mathematical sciences were the chains that bound human thought. But I can breathe now; for those chains are broken.[2]

[2] *Les destinées de la pensée* (1834) ; in H. F. Stewart and A. Tilley's *Romantic Movement in French Literature*, pp. 48 f.

Carlyle was, somewhat less emotionally, echoing the same scorn of mathematics when, in *Sartor Resartus*, he spoke of that "shallow, superficial faculty" of man, the "Arithmetical Understanding."

Such passages, however, do not present any definite philosophical reasons *why* the mathematical sciences should be so contemptuously characterized. But some writers of the period who took the same attitude, did seek to offer logical reasons for it. To both Jacobi and Schelling it seemed simply an obvious corollary of those theorems about the object of any "immediate" (and therefore certain) knowledge which we have reviewed in Lectures II-IV. Thinking by means of general concepts, we were told, cannot give us such knowledge, for concepts are never an immediate experience of *existence*, or Being; they are merely symbols for kinds of potential beings, which we do not actually and directly grasp and possess as within us. They serve well enough for the practically useful procedures of the Understanding, but they do not enable us to attain the goal of the metaphysical quest.

If these premises were accepted, and if it were also assumed that the mathematical sciences consist solely in abstract reasonings about concepts, you could infer that those sciences do not reveal the true nature of "reality." And when, with Schelling, one went on to "prove" that the only object of immediate knowledge, the Ego, is *gar nicht durch zahl bestimmbar,* it seemed evident that the whole realm of the quantitative and numerable is a realm of *un*reality—of the merely "phenomenal," or even of sheer illusion.

But these (supposed) reasons for relegating the categories of quantity and number to that realm were equally pertinent to the category of quality. For we assuredly do have concepts of qualities—not only the class-concept of quality in general, but of specific qualities; and the *gemeine Menschenverstand* is well acquainted with them, has definite and well-discriminated words for many (though not all) of them, *i.e.,* they are far from "ineffable"; and it employs them constantly in its thinking and in its planning for the accomplishment of its everyday utilitarian ends. Nevertheless, these epistemologists saw some radical and philosophically significant contrast between qualities as such and quantities as such, and sometimes made this the essential differentia between the "reality" known by the Reason and the world of mere "appearance" which is the realm of the Understanding.

From the thesis of the purely quantitative nature of conceptual thought, Jacobi deduced the obvious corollary that the whole realm of qualities is foreign to the Understanding.

Of qualities as such we have no concepts, but only intuitions and feelings. Even of our own existence we have only a feeling and no concept. . . . When we say that we have explained a quality, we mean simply that we have reduced it to figure, number, position and motion, have resolved it into those ideas—which is merely a way of saying that in the objective world we have annulled quality altogether.[3]

Schelling, as already indicated, connected this antithesis with the distinction between space and time, and defined time (*i.e.,* "pure" time) as the realm of qualities, and space as an absolute homogeneity entirely destitute of qualitative differentiation. "What has magnitude in time only, we call quality. No one has ever supposed that color, taste and smell are something in space" (a remark resting upon an odd confusion of ideas, especially with regard to color).[4]

By Bergsonian logic also it follows that, since the intellect can deal only with the quantitative, it is incapable of knowing or representing qualities as such. Influenced by the peculiar propensities of the intellect, we tend to treat qualities as if they were reducible to magnitude and figure, and thus as susceptible of geometrical treatment. But in doing this we merely dequalify the qualities, we turn our attention from them, as they are actually given in our experience, to a world of purely quantitative differences outside of us, which

[3] *Werke*, IV, 2 Abt. (1819), p. 149 (note).
[4] *SW*, 1 Abt., 1, *Abhandlung zur Erlauterung*, usw.

science finds it convenient to postulate as the *causes* of our qualitatively irreducible sensations. "The fact is that there is no point of contact between quality and quantity. We can interpret the one by the other, set up the one as the equivalent of the other; but sooner or later we shall have to recognize the conventional character of this assimilation."[5] While, then, the realm of the intellect is that of bare quantity without quality, the realm of intuition is that of absolute quality without quantity or number. *Le monde intérieur*, as Edouard Le Roy puts it, *est celui de la qualité pure*.[6] To another follower of Bergson, Joseph L. P. Segond, this seems the most original and most fundamental of Bergson's discoveries. "It is this antithesis between quantity and quality," he thinks, "which is the principle of all the others" that form the framework of the Bergsonian system; that philosophy is in essence a "constant effort to give its proper place to pure quality, by means of which the real develops."[7] It is to be noted, moreover, that since *le monde intérieur* is, by another principle of Bergsonism, identified with pure time, or duration, an equation of time with quality becomes necessary; so that one of Bergson's favorite names for the reality to be apprehended

[5] *Time and Free Will*, p. 70.
[6] Eng. tr. by V. Benson, p. 77.
[7] *L'Intuition Bergsonienne*, p. 15.

through intuition is *le temps-qualité*. This at times seems to mean only the undeniable proposition that, on the one hand, space in itself is a "pure homogeneity" and involves no notion of qualitative *differences* between its parts and that, on the other hand, the perception of succession would be impossible without qualitative differences in the content of our experience. But this defensible thesis is, of course, irreconcilable with the doctrine of the inapplicability of the notion of number to real duration; and it therefore tends to pass over into a mere identification of time as such with quality as such.

## 2. THE REASON, THE UNDERSTANDING AND THE PRINCIPLE OF CONTRADICTION

We have next to note the emergence of the most radical opposition between the Understanding and Reason or intuition. The reasoning characteristic of ordinary thought and natural science depends upon the setting up of sharp contrasts between things, upon propounding dilemmas and formulating irreconcilable oppositions. The Understanding prides itself upon defining issues sharply and then taking sides. Its entire thinking, in short, is based upon the logical principle of contradiction. But the higher insight of the Reason transcends these oppositions. It is all for embracing both sides of all questions. It makes the dialectical lion lie down with the dialectical lamb; it happily enables you, in speculative matters, to eat your cake and have it too. The Reason thus often declares propositions to be true which, so long as you remain upon the lower level of the Understanding, undeniably *seem* flatly self-contradictory.

That the Schellingian Absolute is a synthesis of contradictory attributes is manifest, especially in the *Identitätslehre*. The "identity of identities," which is here Schelling's name for the Absolute, is all opposed things at once—finite and infinite, real and ideal, temporal and eternal; and equally it is none of these things. The dialectic here is essentially the same as that of Bruno and of Neo-Platonism. Within the original and self-existent Being, the One, there can be no plurality, no division, and no change.

> The essence of the Absolute can only be thought as an absolute, pure, untroubled Identity, *i.e.*, as absolutely excluding all differentiation from its nature. The particular in it is the universal, and the universal the particular; quantity and quality are in it absolutely and inseparably one.[8]

[8] *System des transcendentalen Idealismus* (1800): *SW*, 1, III, 624–25.

Hegel expresses himself, in like manner, in his Schellingian period:

> That these pairs of opposites—be it Self and Nature, pure and empirical consciousness, knowing and being, positing-of-self and positing-of-other, finite and infinite—are posited together in the Absolute: in this antinomy common reflection sees nothing but contradiction. Only the Reason recognizes in this absolute contradiction the truth, namely, that both opposites are posited and both are negated, that neither of them and at the same time both of them *are*.[9]

Friedrich Schlegel too took his fling at this one among the numerous *bêtes noires* of the school: "the principle of contradiction," he declared, "is not even the principle of mere analysis."[10]

It was, of course, in this aspect of the doctrine of knowledge that Hegel found the suggestion of his own characteristic logic. It is worth noting the relation of this logic to the ordinary position of the group whom we have been considering. In the "return to the immediate," which Jacobi and Schelling in some passages had preached as the way to philosophical salvation, Hegel was able to see at best only a half-truth. To *return* to the immediate was to reverse the

[9] *Differenz des Fichteschen und des Schellingschen Systems* (1801), pp. 151–52.

[10] *Athenaeum*, I, 2, p. 22.

movement of Reason, which consists rather in pressing forward to a higher immediacy wherein all the distinctions, all the richness of conceptual content, of the analytic Understanding are included—but also transcended.

> Reason, inasmuch as being life and spirit, it is essentially mediation, is an immediate knowledge only through the sublation of this mediation. It is only a lifeless object of sense that is immediate otherwise than through the mediation of itself with itself. . . . If the immediacy of knowledge is understood in any other sense than this, it is not the immediacy of Reason that is in question, but the kind of immediacy that belongs to a stone. . . . In Jacobi, however, the transition from mediation to immediacy has rather the character of a mere abandonment or avoidance of mediation; . . . indeed, he goes farther, and represents the mediating movement of knowledge as actually obstructive and destructive of the intuition of Reason.[11]

The attempt to reach "the immediate" immediately, that is, by merely ignoring the ordinary logic and by leaving out of consideration the characteristics of ordinary experience, seemed to Hegel to be an example of precisely that excessive subjection to the principle of contradiction from which the philosophers of the newer generation professed to have

[11] Hegel's *Werke* (Berlin, 1835), XVII, 10–11.

escaped. For that attempt was governed precisely by
the assumption that "immediacy" and "mediation"
arc irreconcilable; it simply set up one abstract notion
in opposition to another, and sought to realize the
one by blankly excluding the other. Thus the passion
for the unification of opposites required, when
properly understood, not, indeed, an abandonment,
but a significant transformation, of that other element
which consisted in a revulsion against all indirect or
conceptual modes of acquaintance with Being and a
craving for "the immediate." But for the same reason,
even the overriding of the principles of identity and
contradiction could not be, for Hegel in his final
doctrine, the same simple and direct thing which it
had been for these epistemologists. True, Hegel held,
every category "passes over into its own other,"
"turns into its opposite"; and this seems a contradiction. But on the other hand, the necessity for this
"passing over" lay, as he insisted, in each case in the
fact that the category proved self-contradictory *unless*
it thus embraced its own negation. Thus the principle
of contradiction, so far from being simply abrogated
and disregarded in the Hegelian Logic, is the vital
nerve of the entire dialectic process. "It is easy work
for the Understanding," Hegel writes,

> to show that everything said of the *Idee* [the high-
> est category of the *Logic*] is self-contradictory, The

same charge can, however, equally well be brought home to the Understanding itself, and, in fact, this is already accomplished in the *Idee*. To show this [contradiction in the Understanding] is the work of Reason—a work which is, it is true, not so easy as the work of the Understanding. When the Understanding demonstrates that the *Idee* contradicts itself, because the subjective is subjective only and is always confronted by the obective; . . . because the finite is finite only, the exact antithesis of the infinite, and so on; then the *Logic* proceeds to demonstrate the opposite of all this. It shows that a "subjective" which is subjective only, a "finite" which is finite only, an "infinite" which is infinite only, have no truth, but contradict themselves and pass over into their opposite.[12]

In other words, Hegel does not invite philosophy to reform itself by a bare repudiation of "the fundamental principle of the ordinary logic"; instead, he invites it to use that principle for the undoing of the ordinary logic. It is ostensibly in the name of the laws of the Understanding that he indicts the Understanding.

The result of this procedure, none the less, is that in the end the ordinary logic is effectually undone and the principle of contradiction ruthlessly trodden under foot. It is merely that, by a characteristically

[12] *Encyklopädie der philosophischen Wissenschaften, Erster Teil*, no. 214, in *Werke* VI.

Hegelian paradox, it is, so to say, trodden under its own feet, and lies

Like a god self-slain on his own strange altar.

It is a naïve and erroneous criticism of Hegel to say that he merely flouts the principle of contradiction; but it is equally false and only a little less naïve to say with Croce that he "repudiates only false applications of the principle of contradiction" and that "a contradiction *thought*" after the manner of the Dialectic "is a contradiction overcome."[13] The Dialectic is, indeed, a continuous overcoming of contradictions, yet contradiction in it is never overcome; for it is equally true of it that it is a continuous setting up of contradictions. What one means by a contradiction is a conjunction of ideas which are reciprocally repugnant and irreconcilable from the point of view of ordinary logic; and a contradiction is not logically overcome unless it be shown, in a way that satisfies the ordinary logic, that the ideas in question are *not* mutually repugnant and irreconcilable. But this Hegel makes no pretense of showing. If he had attempted this, indeed, he would have robbed *his* antithesis of Understanding, and Reason of all its point. Reason would in that case have operated upon the same principles as the

[13] *Lebendiges und Totes in Hegel's Philosophie* (Heidelberg, 1909), pp. 25–26.

Understanding; it would have been merely a correct application of those principles, while Understanding would have been a hasty and mistaken application of them. But this is very far from Hegel's view of the relation of the two kinds of logic. In the passage already cited he expressly admits that it *is* easy for the Understanding to point out what *for it* are and must be actual contradictions in the final synthesis of the Dialectic, the Absolute *Idee;* he merely declares that the Reason can always reciprocate the compliment. We are, in fact, left at the end of the *Logic* with nothing better than the unedifying spectacle of the *Vernunft* screaming "You're another" in reply to the reproaches of the *hartnäckige Verstand.* It is not by such means that contradictions are reconciled or reduced to mere seeming.

Schopenhauer may, at first consideration, seem free from this trait of Hegel's logic—or illogic. He speaks with respect, on occasion, of the principle of contradiction and the rest of the four traditional "laws of thought." Yet it must, of course, be remembered that it, like all the other "principles of the Understanding," is, for Schopenhauer too, pertinent only to the phenomenal—to the world of common sense and of natural science—and not to that ulterior realm of Absolute Being with which alone metaphysics is concerned. That, in this realm, contradiction reigns, may be sufficiently seen by a mere collation of the amazingly incongruous attributes which Schopenhauer ascribes to "the Will," as the "Thing-in-itself." And in one passage, written in his later years, Schopenhauer, setting up in its most extreme form the antithesis between a lower and a higher mode of knowledge, expressly declares that the latter is, *from the point of view of the former*, self-contradictory. Thus in the concluding section of the dialogue "On the Doctrine of Life after Death" (*Parerga und Paralipomena*, II), Philalethes, the speaker, who represents the position of the author of the dialogue, is asked by the other interlocutor, Thrasymachus, to answer plainly and briefly the question: "What am I, after my death?" "Everything—and Nothing," is the reply. Thrasymachus not unnaturally complains that this "solution of the problem" is a mere contradiction in terms; to which Philalethes replies that "answering *transcendent* questions in the forms of speech designed for the expression of immanent knowledge may, indeed, lead to contradiction," and he explains this distinction in the following Kantian terms:

> Transcendent knowledge is that which, reaching beyond all possibility of experience, strives to determine the nature of things as they are in themselves; immanent knowledge, on the other hand, is that which keeps within the confines of the possi-

bility of experience, and consequently can tell us only of appearances. Thou, as an individual, endest at death. Only, this individuality of thine is not thy true, essential and ultimate being, but is, rather, a mere outward expression of it; it is not the thing-in-itself, but only its appearance, which is manifested in the form of time and consequently has a beginning and an end. This essence, in itself, on the contrary, knows nought of time, nor of beginning nor end, nor of the limitations of a given individuality; therefore it can be excluded from no individuality, but exists in each and all. In the first sense, therefore, thou becomest, through death, nothing at all; in the second sense, thou art and shalt remain all things. . . . This answer to thy question contains, it is true, a contradiction; for thy life is in *time*, thy immortality in *eternity*—it may accordingly be called an immortality without duration—which is once more, a contradiction. But this is what happens when one attempts to bring the transcendent within the limits of immanent knowledge; the latter suffers a sort of violence, when we misapply it to ends which it was not meant to serve.

This, after all, was more sweepingly, if less plainly, expressed, in the famous concluding passage of the first volume of *The World as Will and Idea,* where the same ultimate identification of the two most glaringly contradictory of all categories—"All" and "Nothing"—is declared to be the last word of Schopenhauer's philosophy.

We freely acknowledge that what remains after the entire abolition of Will is for all those who are still full of will certainly nothing; but, on the other hand, to those in whom the will has turned and negated itself, this our so real world, with all its suns and Milky Ways is—Nothing.

Since I have in the preceding lectures called attention to the numerous and close similarities between the doctrine of Bergson and that of Schelling, it must now be added that the former did not explicitly and unequivocally subscribe to this article of the latter's logic, and when it was formally put before him, he rejected it. Yet the attributes of "real duration" *are* in fact mutually contradictory. As I have already attempted to show, a duration to which the concept of quantity is inapplicable, a temporal succession in which there can be said to be no mutual externality of the successive moments, a "memory" in which the event remembered and the experience of remembering it are simultaneous—these appear to be perfect examples of the assertion of logically irreconcilable predicates of identical subjects. But this issue is sufficiently fully discussed in the Appendix to the present lectures, and the relevant arguments need not be repeated here.

## 3. CREATIVE FREEDOM

We have already recalled that in Kant's philosophy the *Verstand* is distinguished from the *Vernunft* as the "faculty" which, by its very nature, is constrained to a deterministic and mechanistic view of things. However, it seemed to Kant that there can be no moral responsibility without freedom, without something in the individual that is absolutely uncaused; but there can be no freedom in the spatio-temporal world. There all events are completely subject to the law of causality, and therefore every human act is simply the necessary effect of its antecedents. If, then, freedom is to be "saved . . . no other way remains to do so but to attribute it" to a non-temporal self—to the "intelligible character," good or bad which belongs, causelessly and eternally, to each noumenal Ego, yet somehow manifests itself in his temporal behavior as a whole, though without impediment to the determination of each moment of that behavior by antecedent natural causes. For Coleridge this was, not the only, but by far the most important, consequence of the "distinction of Reason and Understanding." Coleridge was deeply sensible that he and other men were miserable sinners; but he did not see how they could

be if their evil acts are necessitated, as in the order
of time they clearly are. The way out Kant seemed to
him to have discovered by his change of venue for the
whole issue from the temporal to the eternal world.
Coleridge thus found in Kant a vindication of the doctrine of Original Sin, which was to him "the fundamental premise of Christianity." Sinfulness is not,
indeed, inherited by us from Adam; the traditional,
mythic form of the doctrine Coleridge thought absurd
and immoral. Sin is literally *original* in every man
because it is inherent in his noumenal Ego which is
out of time and extrinsic to the entire sequence of
natural events. Since the unfortunate empirical self
has never had any opportunity to choose his noumenal
Ego—any more than he had to choose his temporal
ancestors—this seems a curious way of demonstrat-
ing his freedom and responsibility. But it satisfied
Coleridge as a philosophical proof of man's im-
putable iniquity; and from this he deduced the necessity for a supernatural and vicarious means of
redemption, and other articles of the ancient creed.[14]

The philosophers we are here considering, with
some exceptions, were not less eager than Kant to

[14] This part of Coleridge's philosophy and its relation to
Kant's I have dealt with more fully in "Coleridge and Kant's
Two Worlds," in *Essays in the History of Ideas* (Baltimore,
1948), pp. 254 ff.

vindicate freedom; but it was not—for most of them —the same freedom, and the motive for believing in it was not, chiefly, the same motive as Kant's. It was a freedom *in* the temporal order, not one relegated to a supratemporal world; and the usual moralistic and juristic motive for rejecting determinism—the desire to find some way of conceiving of the individual moral agent as somehow *separately* responsible for his deeds —was not their characteristic reason for affirming it. The assumption that a given event in time is fully "explicable" as the "effect" of preceding events might be objected to on three grounds of quite another type.

(a) It implies that all individual events are merely special instances of the operations of general uniform laws. The objection to this would rest, at bottom, on the same ground as another stricture upon the *Verstand*. It seems to deny that any event is unique. Doubtless, events *differ* from one another, and sometimes *look* unique; but when one of these is "explained," in the way in which the Understanding professes to explain it, it proves to be only a new example of a recurrent and invariant process; it is really the same old atoms shuffling about in accordance with the same old laws. The conception of the complete determination of an event by its antecedent thus appears to leave no room for genuine *originality* in the world—originality being the temporal form of

uniqueness or *Eigentümlichkeit*. But *Eigentümlichkeit*
in general, and originality in particular, were concepts dear to the minds of these thinkers; and what is
called the "uniformity of nature" was, when taken
absolutely, antipathetic to those minds because it
seemed incongruous with the possibility of true originality in art, as the achievement of the artistic
genius—and in character.

(b) Aside from this first objection, the notion of
efficient causation *seemed* to imply *pre-*determination;
a happening is all settled before it happens. History
is like the gradual unfolding before us of a scroll; our
*reading* of what is inscribed on the scroll is successive,
but the words inscribed upon it are not successive;
*they* were there all the time. And this idea was peculiarly repellent to many writers because it seemed
to deny to the time-process as a whole any *creative*
potency. If the first morning of creation wrote what
the last dawn of reckoning shall read, then there was
only *one* act of creation; that it took time to disclose
what had already been laid down once for all was a
mysterious oddity of the scheme of things; but nothing except the disclosure was *added* to the content
of the original creation. But Jacobi and Schelling and
others (including Bergson) were convinced that creation keeps going on, that time *is* a creative process,
and, indeed, they tended to use the two terms "time"

and "creation," as equivalent. If this were assumed, it followed, or was construed to follow, that the temporal antecedent does *not* explain the consequent. If it did, history would be like drawing out of a hat rabbits and other things which some magician had already put into it off-stage. But to these metaphysicians—in their temporalistic as distinguished from their eternalistic phase or mood—time is not at all like that; the rabbits are new and surprising rabbits, and there is, in fact, no hat.

(c) The notion of *pre*-determination, finally, may seem to rob the individual moment of human volition of its dramatic poignancy—of, in one sense of a sadly ambiguous word, its significance. What makes such moments seem, so to say, momentous, is the feeling that in them the issue is really open, that something not hitherto settled is actually *getting* settled. It does not add to the excitement of a football game to believe that the result has been prearranged between the coaches or the players. To a spectator who believes this, the game loses the character of a sporting event altogether; does it lose it less if he supposes that it has been prearranged by the Creator, or by the general constitution of nature—that, struggle as they may, the players are not then and there bringing about the outcome, but only explicating a decision that was already "fixed"—whether you call the fixer God, fate, or the totality of antecedent events? A similar reflection could be applied to graver junctures in life than football games. But it was usually characteristic of Schelling and Jacobi and those who later continued their way of thinking, to want their moments momentous, and one not less so than another; to conceive that at every instant there is, at least potentially, "something doing," that the self is *then,* in some absolute sense, "acting" and "striving." But the conception of reality as perpetual *Streben* was, at least seemingly, incongruous with the conception of the complete causal pre-determination of everything; and the Understanding, being by hypothesis committed to the latter conception, was therefore, once more, a faculty which misrepresented the nature of things—though this was admitted to be in some respects a very useful misrepresentation.

I am not presenting these considerations as philosophically cogent; I have been trying only to distinguish some elements in the apparent motivation of the antipathy to determinism. That this strain was inharmonious with other strains, is, I suppose, obvious —*e.g.,* with the eternalistic strain.

I pass now to some illustrations of this disparagement of the Understanding on the ground of its incapacity to recognize "freedom." Jacobi writes:

To the Understanding freedom is wholly inconceivable—and consequently appears to it impossible. . . . It can conceive only of a freedom which is subject to the cosmic law of causal connection . . . not of the only kind of freedom which deserves the name, one which is self-produced and purposive, which *initiates* original works and deeds.[15]

The last phrase is one of the expressions of a sort of equation frequent in Jacobi's philosophy: Consciousness as such is equivalent to freedom, and freedom is equivalent to "invention," the production of the unpredictable and unprecedented.

To be free and to be a spirit (or mind, *Geist*) are one and the same. Where spirit is, there is invention (*Erfindungskraft*), the power of creation (*Schöpfungskraft*), originality, selfhood.

And this freedom, since it involves a possibility of the transcendence of any "law" formulated at any given stage of scientific knowledge, is a sort of "miracle" and a proof that the miraculous is possible.

I too believe for the miracle's sake (*des Wunders wegen*)—for the sake, that is, of the miracle of freedom, which is a continual miracle and has much analogy with the miracle by which Christianity was founded—the descent of the Holy Ghost at Pentecost.[16]

[15] *Werke*, II, 46.
[16] *Ibid.*, VI, 174–75.

Since Jacobi, like Kant, found in man's make-up both the *Verstand* and the *Vernunft*, and since he too applied to men's voluntary actions the principle of the *Verstand* that all events in time "follow one another *nach einer Regel*" in accordance with an invariable law of efficient causation—it might seem that he was committed to determinism. But he, also like Kant, thought it needful to find a way of believing that man as a moral agent is free. *Unlike* Kant, however, he did not assign this freedom to a "noumenal," supersensible Ego which supposedly never acts in time. It was, as he conceived it, a freedom present in each of our temporal acts of volition. To think of one and the same voluntary act of the same individual as completely predetermined and also as completely free may seem to some persons a rather difficult mental feat; but to Jacobi it offered no insuperable difficulty, so long as he kept in mind the distinction between the *Verstand* and the *Vernunft*. As viewed by the former the act is necessitated, as viewed by the latter it is free; and both views are correct—only, the latter view is *more* correct, since the Reason is the "higher" faculty, the sole revealer of ultimate *metaphysical* truth. Realizing, however, that, to some readers not sufficiently instructed in his philosophy, the assertion of these three theorems taken together might still seem unintelligible, not to say self-contradictory,

Jacobi endeavored to elucidate the matter in a short essay of 1799, "On the Inseparability of the Concept of Freedom from the Concept of the Reason."[17]

The precise meaning of my conception of freedom [he writes], can be stated as follows:

I understand by the word freedom that power (*Vermögen*) of man by virtue of which he himself is and by which alone his actions, both internal and external, are performed—by means of which he acts upon things and generates things which did not previously exist (*hervorbringt*). Insofar as he thinks and feels himself to be free, he ascribes solely to *himself* his personal qualities, his science and art, his moral and intellectual character. Only insofar as he sees in himself—in his mind (or spirit, *Geist*), in his intelligence, the originator, the creator, of all these [characteristics and attainments], and not in Nature, does he call himself free —though one part of his constitution (*Wesen*) has been produced in a necessitated manner, and in this part he belongs to and is involved in the general mechanism of Nature. Man, therefore, calls himself free only insofar as in a part of his being he does *not* belong to Nature and is not a product of Nature;

---

[17] *Ueber die Unzertrennlichkeit des Begriffes der Freiheit und Vorsehung von dem Begriffe der Vernunft*, in *Werke*, Bd. II, p. 311 ff. *Vorsehung* here clearly does not mean "providence" in the theological sense. The argument of the essay clearly shows that Jacobi used it to signify "looking-towards-the future."

he is free only insofar as he cuts himself off from
Nature, raises himself above it and dominates it
and, by his faculty of freedom, controls its mechanism and makes it serviceable to himself. The mind
(*Geist*) *alone*, not Nature, is inventive and has design in what it brings forth; it alone imagines and
aspires. The productivity of Nature is blind, devoid
of reason, without purpose or foresight. . . . Thus
Reason and Freedom are inseparably joined together in our consciousness; but not in such a way
that the power to act with freedom (*das freie Vermögen*) is derived from what is called man's rationality, but in the sense that his rationality is
derived from his power to act with freedom.[18]

This passage is not likely to have convinced Jacobi's
more acute-minded readers of the logical possibility
of conceiving of the same temporal event as both
predetermined and "free," *i.e., not* predetermined;
and, indeed, the argument does not seem to have made
that paradox intelligible to Jacobi himself, for in the
end he admits that we cannot "understand" the paradox and, by implication, that we cannot even conceive
of it. For to "understand" any particular event means
to think of its occurrence as conditioned by its relation
to something more general, *i.e.,* by some general law
of nature about the connection (*Verknüpfung*) of
things and events with other things and events. But
this way of thinking is peculiar to the Understanding,

[18] *Op. cit.,* Bd. II, pp. 315–17.

which knows no "Unconditioned." Freedom of the will, however, Jacobi insists, is unconditioned freedom—*unbedingte und unverknüpfte*. It is therefore beyond the comprehension of the Understanding and extraneous to "Nature"; it can only be called a "supernatural" (*übernatürlich*) reality. Of this reality, however, we have an immediate, intuitive certainty. Thus Jacobi's proof of man's freedom appears to rest ultimately upon a dogmatic assertion that he and all men have an indubitable intuition of the truth of a self-contradictory proposition. Reasoning of this sort was unlikely to convince determinists that their doctrine was false.

If this had been all that is to be said about the passage last quoted, it would not have been worth quoting at such length. But the passage is in fact highly significant. For, in spite of the queer illogicality of its principal argument, it also presented—incidentally, as it were—an historically important thesis: It clearly showed (I think) that Kant's way of "saving freedom" was wholly beside the mark. If man's voluntary actions are free, they must be free *when they occur*. But, as we have seen, Kant's so-called freedom consisted (as he defined it) in everyone's having (or being) a timeless or noumenal Ego which has no existence in the phenomenal and therefore temporal world, and which is endowed by the

Creator with a "character" which determines all the individual's temporal acts. For, says Kant, in a man's noumenal existence,

> nothing is antecedent to the determination of his will, but every action [i.e., in time] and in general every modification of his existence, . . . even the whole series of his existence as a sensible being, is, in the consciousness of his supersensible existence, nothing but the *result* . . . of his causality as a noumenon.[19]

This, taken in conjunction with the doctrine about causality of the *Kritik der reinen Vernunft,* means that all human acts have a curious sort of twofold causation: as natural phenomena, they are caused by antecedent natural phenomena, and not free; they are also completely determined by the nature of the particular noumenal self whose acts they are.

Schelling's doctrine of freedom in his earlier writings is not unequivocal, and at times it seems hard to distinguish from what William James used to call a "soft" determinism. But whether the freedom that is in question be of a "sensible" or "supersensible" sort, it is at all events regarded by Schelling as the reality, and necessity as the appearance; and as responsible for this appearance the *Verstand* once more receives from him very hard words.

[19] *Kr. d. pr. V.,* A, 175. Abbott's tr., p. 191.

We have now to speak of that cognition of the Understanding, which flatters itself upon attaining true knowledge (*Wissen*) and consists merely in referring the particular to the universal, and in inferring from cause to effect and *vice versa*. . . . It is the sort of cognition which rests entirely upon mechanical laws, and is dominant in all parts of so-called physical science. . . . To whatever objects it be applied, this mode of cognition never amounts to a knowledge of the Reason, but only of the Understanding. . . . That a knowledge which consists in inferring from effect to cause, which seeks to know a first principle through that of which it is the first principle, the original through the derivative—that such a procedure can never bring us to anything that exists in itself and of itself, is as clear as it is that it can never enable us to know what it regards as the cause in its *intrinsic* nature, apart from its effects. . . . It is not that this sort of cognition, which we may, in a word, call empiricism, . . . is sometimes more and sometimes less objectionable; it is wholly false, by its very principle, and a perpetual and inexhaustible source of error. Not its form only must be altered; the entire view must be reversed, and transformed in its principles, before there can arise a true knowledge of the objects which this sort of cognition takes for its own. . . . What greater superstition can there be, than to believe that the things which in physics, *e.g.*, or chemistry, are represented as causes actually produce the effects [with which those sciences deal]?[20]

Bergson similarly dwells upon the thesis that intellect is constitutionally incapable of comprehending freedom. It necessarily links together all events, outer or inner, in the nexus of efficient causation; and "the more sharply the idea of efficient causality is defined in our mind, the more it takes the form of mechanical causality."[21] Thus the world of mechanism, and of mechanism alone, is the world in which the intellect finds itself at home. But the world of mechanism is not the real world; it is only a fiction serviceable to the requirements of action. Life and consciousness are essentially free; and once again, therefore, they elude the intellect's grasp. The essence of their freedom consists, for Bergson too, in their power to "create," to bring into existence the absolutely novel and unpredictable; he likes to speak of *le temps-créateur*. The fundamental reason for the inability of the intellect to think freedom is its incapacity "to admit complete novelty." Its chief func-

[20] *SW*, I, Abt. IV, *Fernere Darstellungen aus dem System der Philosophie* (1802). It should be added that in his *Wesen der menschlichen Freiheit* (1809), Schelling admits a "*moral necessity*" in all choice, divine or human, and rejects the freedom of indifference.

[21] Creative Evolution, p. 44.

tion is to foretell the future upon the assumption that the past, the already-given, furnishes the key to the future; and its typical expression is the mechanistic hypothesis, simply because the essence of that hypothesis *is* the assumption that "*all* is given" *ab initio*, that the world is made up of a constant number of component units, unalterable in their constitution and changing their relations only in accordance with unchanging laws, a knowledge of which would have made possible the prediction of the entire cosmic drama. This hypothesis, however, is not, for Bergson, wholly false; we should be in a bad fix if it were, since we could never infer from the past what any of the future effects of our present action will be. But he contends that there remains at every moment a *marginal* freedom; each present adds *something* which the past knew not of; and therefore the future cannot be assumed to be completely predictable.

## 4. CREATIVE EVOLUTION

From the outset Schelling was chiefly (I do not say, solely) preoccupied with two distinct theses. The first was primarily epistemological; it was the theory of knowledge of which the premises have already been outlined in the preceding lectures, the famous and for a time widely influential thesis that we have two cognitive faculties, the Reason and the Understanding, of which the former is the organ of metaphysical knowledge of what really and certainly exists, while the latter is merely the organ of natural science and is only useful for the guidance of our bodily actions. When he was explicating the epistemological thesis about the *Vernunft* and the *Verstand*, Schelling attempted to prove that the reality known by the Reason is necessarily immutable and timeless.[22] But what is now necessary to add is that at an equally early period of his philosophizing he was developing precisely the opposite thesis: that *nothing* that exists, including ourselves and even God, is immutable.

"Nature," writes Schelling in 1799, "struggles against all permanence," for no product which she has at any time achieved can exhaust her infinite creative energy. Into each of them, it is true, the whole power of Nature (*die Kraft der ganzen Natur*) is in a sense poured out; but just for this reason—because there is, as it were, a latent pressure towards infinity in it —no finite thing can remain unchanged; "it must be only apparently finite, but in reality in endless evolution (*Entwicklung*); . . . in each of them lies the germ of a universe."[23]

[22] See pp. 77 ff.
[23] *Naturphilosophie*, *SW*, 1, III, 290 (1799).

Of the incongruity between the conception of the eternal yet all-comprehending reality and this conception of a reality which is essentially a creative energy manifesting itself gradually in a temporal process, Schelling is aware; and he seeks to eliminate it by distinguishing between that which is logically possible but not now existent, and that which is not only possible but also actually "realized." In a sense, the former *is,* as the Schoolmen would have said, only *in potentia* and not *actu.* And what goes on in time is a *Realwerdung,* a becoming actual, an acquisition of existence by what, apart from the temporal process, would remain, as it were, frustrate and incomplete, so long as it falls short of the existential status. The "timeless" Absolute is thus, after all, made subordinate, in *The Philosophy of Nature,* to time; for it (Schelling postulates) cannot "realize" itself all at once. The concept, he writes, of "an absolute productivity implies that such a productivity is infinite; but this is, so far, merely an infinity in idea, not in actuality. The absolute productivity must therefore pass over into an empirical world of nature, and its infinity in idea into an empirical infinity." But in experience a literal, completed infinite is impossible; in other words, "an empirical infinity" can only be "an endless becoming." Now "the original infinite series, the ideal of all such series, is time, in which our intellectual infinity unfolds itself."

This does not tell us in what concrete fashion the actual or "empirical" unfolding of the possibles in time, their *Entwicklung* or *Evolution* (Schelling employs both terms) takes place. But it was in fact *towards* the theory of organic evolution in its present sense that he was being led by these abstract metaphysical or dialectical reasonings. A year or two earlier he had already attributed to the "Spirit of Nature"—*i.e.*, the *anima mundi*, mentioned in Lecture four—a "steady and undeviating march towards the organic": and this, he declared,

> clearly betrays a vigorous impulsion (*einen regen Trieb*) which, always struggling, as it were, with inanimate matter, now triumphs over it, now is subjected to it—breaks through it now in freer, now in more restricted forms. It is the universal *Spirit* of nature, which by degrees gives form to matter. From the bit of moss, in which the mark of the organic is almost imperceptible, to the most exalted form, which seems to have shaken off the chains of matter altogether, one and the same impulsion rules—working towards one and the same purposive Ideal, striving to express *in infinitum* one and the same model, the pure form of our mind (*die reine Form unseres Geistes*). It would be at least one step towards a scientific understanding of

organic nature if one could show that the graded sequence of all organized beings has formed itself (*sich gebildet habe*) through a gradual development of one and the same organization. The fact that our experience makes us acquainted with no transformations in nature, no transition from one form into another, is no proof against this possibility (though, indeed, the metamorphoses of many insects, and, if every bud is a new individual, also the metamorphoses of plants, may be cited as at least analogous phenomena). For a defender of this hypothesis could reply that the changes to which organic as well as inorganic nature is subject, can (until a general static condition of the organic world comes about) take place in ever longer periods for which our periods . . . can afford no measure—the former being so great that as yet no experience has been long enough to span one of them.

But for Schelling this does not imply the transformation of species.

There is an eternal model, which is expressed in every plant; for, however far back we go, we find that the plant, *i.e.*, a given species arises only from itself and returns to itself; only the matter in which it is expressed pays the tribute of mortality (*Vergänglichkeit*); but the form of the organism (the very concept of it) is indestructible.[24]

[24] *SW*, 1, I, 387 (1796–97).

But even if **Schelling's** temporalism, his thesis that the whole creation is a gradual process of the evolution and enrichment of reality, be accepted, could this thesis be true of the Creator? Is it also true that God has evolved and is evolving in time from a lower and more meager kind of existence to a higher and fuller kind? This latter and revolutionary thesis Schelling asserted quite clearly in the following passage from *Ueber das Wesen der menschlichen Freiheit* (1809):

> Has creation a final goal? And if so, why was it not reached at once? Why was the consummation not realized from the beginning? To these questions there is but one answer: Because God is *Life*, and not merely being. All life has a *fate*, and is subject to suffering and to becoming. To this, then, God has of his own free will subjected himself .... Being is *sensible* only in becoming. In being as such, it is true, there is no becoming; in the latter, rather, it is itself posited as eternity. But in the actualization (of being) through opposition there is necessarily a becoming. Without the conception of a humanly suffering God—a conception common to all the mysteries and spiritual religions of the past—history remains wholly unintelligible.[25]

This novel thesis was not allowed to pass unchallenged. Jacobi published in 1811 an essay *Von den göttlichen Dingen und Ihrer Offenbarung* which

[25] *Schellings Werke*, herausg. von A. Weiss (1907), III, 499.

was largely devoted to attacking this contention of
Schelling. "There can," he wrote, "be only two principal classes of philosophers: those who regard the
more perfect (*Vollkommnere*) as derived from, as
gradually developed out of, the less perfect, and those
who affirm that the most perfect being was first, and
that all things have their source in him; that the first
principle of all things was a moral being, an intelligence willing and acting with wisdom—a Creator—
God." Jacobi finally took his stand upon what he regarded as an elementary and obvious principle of
ordinary logic: that something cannot come from
nothing, nor the superior from the inferior. Such a
philosophy as Schelling's, in fact, is, Jacobi asserts,
a direct contradiction of a law of formal logic. For,
as he observes—the observation is a commonplace of
Platonistic theology—the relation of God to the
world may, among other things, be conceived as the
relation of a logical *prius*, a *Beweisgrund* or reason,
to its consequences, the implications deducible from
it. But "always and necessarily a *Beweisgrund* must
be *above* that which is to be proved by means of it,
and must subsume the latter under it; it is from the
*Beweisgrund* that truth and certitude are imparted to
those things which are demonstrated by means of it;
from it they borrow their reality."

Schelling replied in 1812 in his *Denkmal der*

*Schrift von den göttlichen Dingen* in which he did not retract the thesis which he had already expressed but stated it with even more emphasis.

I posit God [says Schelling] as the first and the last, as the Alpha and the Omega; but as Alpha he is not what he is as Omega, and in so far as he is only the one—God "in an eminent sense"—he can not be the other God, in the same sense, or, in strictness, be called God. For in that case, let it be expressly said, the unevolved (*unentfaltete*) God, *Deus implicitus,* would already be what, as Omega, the *Deus explicitus* is.[26]

Upon what grounds, in the face of Jacobi's objections, does Schelling justify this evolutionary theology? First of all on the ground that it accords with the actual character of the world of our experience, as that character is disclosed to our everyday observation and to the more comprehensive vision of natural science. On the face of it, the world is precisely a system in which the higher habitually develops out of the lower, fuller existence out of emptier. The child grows into a man, the ignorant become learned; "not to mention that nature itself, as all know who have the requisite acquaintance with the subject, has gradually risen from the production of more meagre and inchoate creatures to the production of more perfect

[26] *SW*, I, Abt. 8, 81.

and more finely formed ones." A process which is constantly going on before our eyes can hardly be the inconceivability which Jacobi had made it out to be. The new philosophy had simply interpreted the general or "ultimate" nature of things, and their order in being, in the light of the known nature and sequences of all particular things with which we are acquainted. The "ordinary theism," defended by Jacobi, had, on the contrary, given us "a God who is alien to nature and a nature that is devoid of God—*ein unnatürlicher Gott und eine gottlose Natur.*"

Again, Schelling observes, the fact of evil, the imperfection of the world, is irreconcilable with the belief that the universe proceeds from a being perfect and intelligent *ab initio*. Those who hold this belief "have no answer when they are asked how, from an intelligence so clear and lucid, a whole so singularly confused (even when brought into *some* order) as the world can have arisen." In every way, then, Schelling finds the picture of reality which accords with the facts is that of a more or less confused and troubled ascent towards fuller and higher life; and the only admissible conception of God is that which is in harmony with this picture. Nor has the contrary view, he declares, the religiously edifying and consoling character to which it pretends. For it "derives the not-good from the Good, and makes God, not the source and

potentiality of the good, but the source and potentiality
of the not-good." Conceived—as in the theology of
absolute becoming it is conceived—as a good in the
making, *als ein ins Gute Verwandelbares,* evil or imperfection itself is not the hopeless and senseless piece
of reality which it must be if conceived as good in
the *un*making, as a lapse from a perfection already
realized. The God of all the older theology, moreover, had been a God eternally complete, "ready-
made once for all," as Schelling puts it. But no
conception could be more barren and unprofitable
than this; for it is really the conception of a "dead
God," not of the God that lives and strives in nature
and in man. It is inconceivable, Jacobi had declared,
that life should arise out of death, being out of non-
being, higher existence out of lower. Is it, then, asked
Schelling, easier to conceive that death should arise
out of life? "What could move the God who is not a
God of the dead but of the living, to produce death.
Infinitely more conceivable is it that out of death—
which cannot be an absolute death, but only the death
which has life concealed within it—life should arise,
than that life should pass over into, should lose itself
in, death." Jacobi's error, however,—Schelling observes—is a natural consequence of the logical doctrine of the older philosophy from which he never
fully emancipated himself; it is, indeed, the crowning

example of the pernicious results in metaphysics of the acceptance of the Wolffian theory of knowledge, which based everything upon the logical Principle of Identity, and regarded all certain judgments as "analytical." According to this view, says Schelling —not with entire historical accuracy—"all demonstration is merely a progression in identical propositions, there is no advance from one truth to a different one, but only from the same to the same. The tree of knowledge never comes to bloom or to fruitage; there is nowhere any *development*." But true philosophy and truly objective science are not a chanting of tautologies. Their object is always a concrete and living thing; and *their* progress and evolution is a progress and evolution of the object itself. "The right method of philosophy is an ascending, not a descending, one"; and its true axiom is precisely opposite to that pseudo-axiom which Jacobi had enunciated:

> Always and necessarily that from which development proceeds (*der Entwicklungsgrund*) is lower than that which is developed; the former raises the latter above itself and subjects itself to it, inasmuch as it serves as the matter, the organ, the condition, for the other's development.

It is—as has too little been noted by historians— in this introduction of a radical evolutionism into metaphysics and theology, and in the attempt to revise even the principles of logic to make them harmonize with an evolutional conception of reality, that the historical significance of Schelling chiefly consists. The question at issue in his controversy with Jacobi is, indeed, as he clearly recognized and emphatically declared, one of the most fundamental and momentous of all philosophical questions, both by its relation to many other theoretical problems, and also by its consequences for the religious consciousness. Schelling's thesis meant not only the discarding of a venerable and almost universally accepted axiom of rational theology and metaphysics, but also the emergence of a new mood and temper of religious feeling.

For Schelling himself, however, the implication of this doctrine of a God-in-the-making could not be simply a blandly cheerful evolutionary meliorism. The progress of the world, the gradual manifestation or self-realization of God, is a struggle against opposition; since the full possibilities of being were not realized all at once, and are not yet realized, there must in the original nature of things be some impediment, some principle of retardation, destined to be triumphed over, indeed, but not without suffering and temporary defeats. The Life-Force advances fumblingly, by trial and error. There is a tragic element in cosmic and in human history; the world-process is *ein Wechselspiel von Hemmen und von Streben.*[27]

The questions at issue between Jacobi and Schelling show themselves again in the philosophy of Bergson, which appears to have passed through at least three phases.[28] (a) In the first phase, Bergson, as we have seen, conceived of the "genuinely real" as eternal and immutable. (b) In what is perhaps his most widely read volume, *L'evolution creatice* (1908), Bergson seems to represent the whole of reality, including divinity itself, as temporal and progressive. Bergson's conception of the most fundamental force in the universe, the *élan vital,* is described as an urge, an impulsion, anterior to and independent of the bodies of which it takes possession. It makes not only for novelty, for increasing variation in definite directions, for expansion, but also for individuation. It drives on insatiably and unwearyingly towards more life, fuller and more diversified. It more and more, as Bergson's characterization progresses, comes to resemble the Schopenhauerian *Wille zum Leben,* on the more posi-

---

[27] For a more comprehensive treatment of the Schelling and Jacobi controversy see *The Great Chain of Being,* Chapter XI, from some of which the above is taken, especially pp. 323, 324, 325.

[28] I do not consider here Bergson's later work, *The Two Sources of Morality and Religion.*

tive side of that versatile entity.[29] For the *élan vital* too is defined as of the nature of volition. This vital impulsion has a sort of purposiveness, though a purposiveness without prevision or conscious design. Life is like a blind giant; it runs up many blind alleys, diverges a thousand times from its straight course, yet upon the whole forges ahead in one prevailing direction. When thwarted in its endeavor towards its characteristic though unforeseen ends—as it is constantly thwarted by its eternal antagonist, inert matter—it is endlessly fertile in devices for overcoming opposition or circumventing obstructions. It is, moreover, not a power existing separately in individual living things and operating in them disconnectedly; rather is it a cosmic force in and by which all individual organisms live and move and have their being, and to whose vaster strivings all their groaning and travailing are but incidents. And thus—to quote once more the now celebrated passage which concludes the third chapter of *Creative Evolution:*

> With this doctrine we feel ourselves no longer isolated in humanity, humanity no longer isolated in the nature that it dominates. As the smallest grain of dust is bound up with our entire solar system, drawn along with it in that undivided move-

[29] See my article "Schopenhauer as an Evolutionist," in *Forerunners of Darwin* (Baltimore, 1959), pp. 415–37.

ment of descent which is materiality itself, so all
organized beings, from the humblest to the highest,
from the first beginnings of life to the time in which
we are, and in all places as in all times, do but
evidence a single impulsion, the inverse of the
movement of matter, and itself indivisible. All the
living hold together, all yield to the same tre-
mendous urge. The animal takes its stand upon the
plant, man bestrides animality, and the whole of
humanity, in space and in time, is one immense
army galloping beside and before and behind each
one of us in an overwhelming charge which is able
to beat down all resistance and to overcome the
most formidable obstacles—perhaps even death.

But now is this characterization of the *élan vital*
to be understood as equivalent to a definition of the
Being usually called God? Bergson argues with much
force and emphasis in that volume against the assumption which, as he says, "lies at the base of ancient"
—more correctly, of all Platonistic—"philosophy:
that there is more in the motionless than in the moving, and that we pass from immutability to becoming
by way of diminution or attenuation." He argues with
no less energy against the tendency of post-Kantian
idealists to regard the forms which succeed one
another as deducible "directly from the one complete
being which they are supposed to manifest"; this, he
insists, "is to deny to derivation all efficacy." Clearly,

the philosophical undertaking to which he appears to commit himself, that of construing reality through and through as a thing *se faisant,* and not *tout fait*—would preclude the recognition of any self-sufficient and perfect reality either transcendent of time, or temporally or logically antecedent to the evolutionary process. The reader of *L'evolution creatice* would, I am sure, be likely to suppose that the term *élan vital* was his equivalent of the term God. Indeed, in one sentence he definitely enunciates and adopts the conception of a God in the making. As defined by the argument which he has presented, writes Bergson, "God has nothing of the already made; he is unceasing life, action, freedom." And it is in this life, we seem to be told, that we human individual persons subsist. So in his *L'Intuition philosophique* Bergson declares that "human consciousness is affiliated to a vaster and higher consciousness. The forces which are at work in all things, we feel also in ourselves; whatever be the inner nature of that which is and which is making itself, we are *of* it." It is, then, a species of evolutionary pantheism which one would suppose to be the philosophy of religion implied by *L'evolution creatice.*

(c) But in 1912, to the surprise of many, Bergson gave a reply to an inquiry on the subject which at first seems to suggest that it is *not* such a philosophy of religion which he holds or had intended to con-

vey. A Belgian Jesuit, Father de Tonquédec, published in the *Études,* the scholarly review maintained
by members of the Society of Jesus, an article on the
religious aspect of Bergson's philosophy in which he
pointed out that Bergson had, after all, given an
ambiguous answer to the theological problem of the
relation of God to the world. His philosophy re-
peatedly bids us "reascend the current of life to its
source." But is that source of the same nature as,
and identical in being with, the movement which
proceeds from it, "or is there *dans les régions trans-
cendantes* something radically distinct from even the
purest current of created life?" There are texts in
Bergson's books, and aspects of his reasoning, Father
de Tonquédec observed, which readily suggest the
former interpretation, the conclusion that for him
"there cannot be substantial identity between life and
its source." But there are many other expressions,
and other implications of the Bergsonian argument,
which appear to demand the contrary construction.
Thus, as Father de Tonquédec concluded, one cannot determine, "in reading Bergson, whether 'God' is
a name given to a reality which will *become* the
world, or whether the world designates *quelque chose
ou quelqu'un de plus reculé dans l'audelà.*"

Being thus invited to define his theological position
with more explicitness, Bergson replied in two letters

to his critic, which have since been published in the
*Études;* and in these he seemed to authorize the former
of the two interpretations mentioned by Father de
Tonquédec.

I speak of God [he wrote] as the source from which
proceed, one after another, as an effect of his
liberty, the currents or *élans* of which each constitutes a world; he therefore remains distinct from
these and it is not of him that one can say that 'most
often it comes to a stop' or that it is 'at the mercy
of the materiality which it has taken upon itself.'
Finally the argument by which I establish the im-
possibility of non-existence is not at all directed
against the existence of a cause transcending the
world; on the contrary, I have explained that it has
reference to the Spinozistic conception of being.
The outcome of it is simply that *some*thing must
have always existed. On the nature of this something, to be sure, it expresses no positive conclusion;
but it in no way says that what has always existed
is the world itself and the rest of the book says
explicitly the contrary.[30]

In a later letter, Bergson goes so far as to represent his
entire philosophical work as constituting a long, connected proof of the existence of God, and of an external or transcendent God, not one with the world

[30] I may add that Bergson neglects at this point to give refer-
ences to the passages in his book in which this is explicitly said.

which he creates. "The considerations," Bergson writes, "which I have set forth in my *Essay on the Immediate Data of Consciousness* culminated by bringing to light the fact of liberty; those in *Matter and Memory* made palpable, I trust, the reality of spirit [or mind]; those in *Creative Evolution* presented creation as a fact. From all this there clearly emerges the idea of a God who is a creator and who is free; who generates at once matter and life; and whose creative effort continues, on the side of life, through the evolution of species and the formation of human personalities. From all this, consequently, there results the refutation of monism and of pantheism in general."

That Bergson has not formally excluded the possibility of a transcendent deity, prior and external to the evolving world, and setting it in motion without being implicated in that motion, is true enough. But had he, as a matter of fact, offered anything remotely resembling a demonstration, or a serious attempt at a demonstration, of the theological conclusion to which in the letters cited he represents his entire course of reasoning as tending. If you turn to the particular pages of *Creative Evolution* to which he especially refers as giving his conception of God,[31] you will, indeed, discover that he there figuratively describes

[31] Eng. tr., pp. 247–51.

"God," with a somewhat Dantesque boldness of meta-
phor, as "a center from which worlds shoot out like
rockets in a fireworks display." But he adds that we
must not—as the intellect tends to do—represent this
center as a *thing*, but as a *continuité de jaillissement*,
a continuous shooting out; and there immediately follow the significant words already quoted; "God thus
defined has nothing of the already made; he is unceasing life, action, freedom." And the nature of this
creative activity, we are further told, "we experience
ourselves whenever we act freely." Now in this simili-
tude, I think you will agree, there is *not* suggested the
conception of a transcendent deity in the Jesuit
theologian's sense—the term God is distinctly not
applied to something in "the transcendent regions distinct from the purest current of created life," and
there is no approach to the assertion that there "cannot be any substantial identity between life and its
source." On the contrary, the identity in nature between all life and its perennial source is plainly
affirmed. In the entire passage in question Bergson
simply gives the name of God to the inexhaustible
reservoir of vital energy in which he believes; but he
warns us that we must not be misled by the figure—
the reservoir is not a receptacle containing this energy,
it is not a reserved quantity of life-force kept tempo-
rarily in an inactive condition until needed; it is just

the endless "shooting out" of life itself, regarded as inexhaustible—viewed, so to say, under its aspect of inexhaustibility.

No, I am afraid that in his correspondence with Father de Tonquédec, Bergson has added a gloss to his published doctrine which does not, as it is likely to be understood, faithfully render the natural sense and dominant tendency of that doctrine. His books contain no real "refutation of monism and of pantheism in general"; and, so long as he is speaking of a world of Becoming that really becomes, his God is simply that Becoming—or, if you please to use such expressions, is the soul or ever-pulsing heart of it.

Bergson, then, is here expressing in this phase of his doctrine essentially the same conception as that of Schelling. And for contemporary religious thought the relatively more novel and the more influential aspect of Bergson's teaching is certainly to be found in his conception of creative evolution, and in those expressions of his which suggest as the central feature of a philosophy of religion the conviction that the whole evolutionary process is the manifestation of an expansive life-force, inexhaustible and ever active, yet not omnipotent and never at the goal of its activity; a power which manifests itself at first in low and feeble forms of life, and even in its ascent frequently deviates from its true course, but always extricates itself, always continues to produce fuller and richer and more various and more highly individualized forms of life, culminating thus far in man, and by this culmination revealing the meaning and main direction of that blind, unknowing striving which has from the first urged life unceasingly upward.

# Bergson on "Real Duration"

The pertinent part of the letter of Bergson referred to at the end of Lecture III is here quoted in translation—though the translation does not do justice to the felicity of the French original.

The difficulties which you find in my description of duration are doubtless due to the fact that it is hard, if not impossible, to express in words a thing which is repugnant to the very essence of language. I can only attempt to *suggest* it. Duration is indivisible: but this nowise implies that the past and the present are simultaneous. On the contrary, duration is essentially succession; only it is a succession which does not imply a "before" and "after" external to one another. You will be able to have a clear feeling of all this if, while listening to a melody, you allow yourself to be lulled by the sound—at the same time making abstraction from all the visual images which, in spite of yourself, will tend to modify the auditory perception—visual images of notes of music written on paper, or musi-

cal instruments beginning and ceasing to play, *etc.*
You will become conscious that the melody progresses, that it is a movement or a change, that
it is a thing which lasts, and which, consequently,
is not a simultaneity; but that, in this melody, the
past is incorporated with (*fait corps avec*) the
present, and constitutes with it an indivisible
whole. It is only by an effort of reflection that,
subsequently turning back upon this indivisible
whole once constituted, you represent it to yourself
as a simultaneity, because of its indivisibility:—
which leads you to have a *spatial* image of it,
capable of being cut up into distinct terms, de-
composable into a "before" and "after", which then
would be juxtaposed. No doubt this melody, even
in pure duration, seems divisible in the sense that
at any given moment it may come to a stop; but if it
actually came to a stop, we should have a *different melody*, which would itself be indivisible.
When we pronounce a phrase all at once, without
punctuation, we have, once more, the clear feeling
of a succession without before or after, the feeling
of a *solid*—by which I mean an indivisible—duration. Now, in precisely the degree in which we
make a greater effort of attention to resume possession of ourselves, in that degree we tend to perceive our inner life which "expands" without ever
permitting divisions, in absolutely the same way as
a continuing melody. Our inner life, from the beginning to the end, is thus an indivisible continuity,
—and it is this that I call our duration. It is suc-

cession, but succession without distinct and numerical multiplicity, that is to say, *pure* succession.

When one has once gained this experience one finds many great philosophical difficulties fall to the ground. For the rest, it is quite natural that when one has convinced oneself of the indivisibility of the fundamental duration, one should continue to give attention to a duration more or less spatialized—for the greater convenience of thought and of life. But I feel, for my part, incapable of philosophizing, except by bringing myself back to this fundamental duration. It is because of their failure to do this that the philosophers have failed to constitute a philosophy of change, even when they have felt that change was the true reality. They have talked of change, but I doubt whether they have had a perception of it. And it is because they have taken it under an artificial form that they have not succeeded in solving the enigmas of philosophy, to which, none the less, it affords us the key. I am quite sure that "temporalism" will end by establishing itself upon this basis—under penalty, if it does not, of remaining fruitless and of finding itself again confronted, in another form, with all the antinomies of the traditional philosophy.

To this should be added a passage in which Bergson gave an express answer to the question whether he himself recognized a contradiction in the attributes which he ascribes to "time."

If I say to a philosopher that the immediate and naïve experience of the succession of the notes of a melody does not imply the perception of a "before" and "after," although it also is in no sense the perception of a simultaneity, the thing seems to him "self-contradictory" only because he takes the word "succession" in the sense which he will *afterwards* give to it, when his perception is no longer *naïve* but has been translated into a spatial and intellectual form. This translation once made, "succession" becomes synonymous with "distinction of a before and after," and it consequently becomes self-contradictory to speak of a succession in which before and after are not distinguished. But it would suffice, in order to avoid this contradiction, merely to give another name to the perception of succession in its naïve and primitive form. Call it, if you please, a perception of the "non-simultaneous" or of the "moving"; and reserve, if you will, the name of "succession" for the form (in appearance more clear because it is more social) in which this perception of the non-simultaneous or of the moving, when the spatial translation of it permits us to take with respect to it the double point of view of "before" and "after," is clearly distinguished. This done, the contradiction at once disappears. I say, then, that real duration in no sense implies contradiction. It becomes contradictory only for one who proceeds as I have just said, and treats time as space; but in that case it is he who created the contradiction. In a general way I consider the "principle of contradiction" as a principle of universal validity. But contradiction or non-contradiction can pertain only to our manner of formulating the real; as for reality itself, as it is immediately given to us, before being treated by the discursive intellect, it is neither contradictory nor non-contradictory. We ought to formulate things in such a manner as to avoid contradiction: that is always possible, and it is in this sense that the principle of contradiction has a universal validity. But one has never the right to oppose to an immediate perception of the real, the argument that it is self-contradictory, for the contradiction can come only from a defective way of formulating it.

Bergson thus finds the empirical *samples* of the intuition of duration in two kinds—or rather, two instances of a single kind—of common experience; the correctness of his description of these, he believes, anyone can easily verify for himself. The two are the perception of a melody—of a temporal musical pattern—and the pronouncing of a phrase "all at once," by which he presumably meant, "very rapidly." About these, at least, there is no mystery. They are everyday occurrences, about the character of which Bergson offers his own introspective report; and he invites us to compare it with the results of our own introspection.

If we do so, we shall first of all, I think, recognize a fact which may be, and probably is, the root of Bergson's account of "duration"; whether that account accurately expresses the fact is another question. It is true—and is, indeed, a commonplace of the psychology books, in their chapters on time-perception —that in the apprehension of, *e.g.*, a melody or a rhythm, the notes or beats are, and must be, apprehended together, yet not together in the way in which the parts of a spatial pattern, *e.g.*, a picture, are. Physically the stimuli, *i.e.*, the sound-waves are, of course, successive; physiologically, their effects are successive, *i.e.*, the actions of the receptor mechanisms occur one after another; but the notes are apprehended as integrated into a *Gestalt*, all the elements of which are, in some sense, present to consciousness at once. If it were not so, no melody would be perceived; for simply to hear a succession of separate notes is not to recognize a melody. But it is equally true that no melody would be recognized if the notes were given as simply simultaneous; for it is of the essence of the experience that the notes should be apprehended as having a temporal order, and the entire series as characterized by transition and "flow."

Nor is this seemingly paradoxical dual character peculiar to the perception of melodies or rhythms; it belongs to any perception of succession. Kant long ago pointed out that a succession of perceptions is not the same thing as a perception of succession. To experience succession is to be conscious of a contrast between at least two bits of content of awareness—of the passing over from one to the other, or the substitution of one *for* the other; and this also means that both must—again, in *some* sense—be present for awareness together.

Such, then, are the familiar psychological facts about time-perception which may reasonably be supposed to have given the cue for Bergson's description of "real duration." But does his description accurately correspond to the facts? In considering this question, we may well be guided by his judicious remark that if there appears a contradiction in an account of an immediate perception, "the contradiction can come only from a defective way of formulating it." Now Bergson's report, in the first place, still, I must confess, appears to me to be, at the crucial point, contradictory. To speak of a "succession which does not imply a 'before' and 'after' external to one another" is to assert and deny the same thing of the same subject of discourse, namely, a supposedly given experience. The same is true of the alternative proposition that, in the experience in question, past and present are given as "non-simultaneous," or "moving," yet still without being given as "before" and "after" one another. Of course, if the experience is really "repugnant to the very essence of language," we ought not to talk, to use words, about it at all; and if you don't talk, you are in no danger of contradicting yourself. But since Bergson *is* using words to tell us of the nature of the intuition of duration, we may legitimately require that the words, taken together, should convey a meaning—*i.e.*, should be free from contradiction.

But the ultimate appeal in the matter is, admittedly, to introspection; the crucial question is: What do you find that the perception of a melody, or of succession in general, is experienced *as*? And on this every man must report for himself. Let us, for brevity, limit the question to Bergson's own example of the perception of a melody. For myself, I can only say that I have never experienced a melody in which the notes had no "distinct and numerical multiplicity," or were not apprehended as in the relation of "before" and "after." I seem to myself, indeed, to hear each separate note, one after the other, though, while hearing each, I may be continuously aware of the total musical unit, or pattern, of which it is a part. If the melody is wholly new to me, I do not become aware of this pattern in its entirety until the last note sounds, unless, when the melody has partly run its course, I seem to "catch" it by anticipating, perhaps erroneously, the notes I have not yet heard. That Bergson's experience was really the same seems implied by his remark that "at any given moment the melody may come to a stop; but if it actually came to a stop, we should have a different melody." Only a *sequence* of which the units are experienced as before and after one another *can* "come to a stop"; a temporally "indivisible" unity would have all its elements present at once, and there could be no question of stopping or not stopping. The result of my own introspection thus seems to be confirmed, unconsciously, by Bergson himself; and I am thereby encouraged to surmise that it would also be confirmed by others.

As little, then, in the perception of a melody as in any verifiable case of memory, do we find a mode of actual human experience to which Bergson's description of *la durée réelle* is applicable. We have, it is true, seen in such perception a peculiarity which enables us to understand how he can have been led to that description, but this peculiarity he has misinterpreted. In consequence of an insufficient introspective analysis he has overlooked distinctions actually given as elements in the type of experience in question; and as a result of missing these distinctions, he has been left struggling in a morass of sheer self-contradiction. Thus the verifiable empirical example of the "metaphysical intuition" in which the mutual externality, the before-and-afterness, of the moments of our temporal existence is transcended, still eludes us.

It may be objected, however, that the same contradiction appears in this account of time perception as in Bergson's. For I have said that, in any such perception, at least two items of content—for example, notes—recognized as earlier and later, and therefore as "mutually external," must nevertheless be, in *some* sense, present together for awareness. But the solution is that they are not experienced as present in the same sense of "present." There is a happy phrase of Dewey's which succinctly describes the most essential and pregnant peculiarity of our temporal experience. Things, he observes, can be "present-*as-absent*." Even in what the psychologists call "primary memory," the basis of all perception of succession, this is illustrated. In the specious present which is called "now," part of the sensory or other content of which I was aware a moment ago is still present; but it is present as "old stuff," more or less clearly discriminated from the "new stuff" which is the fresh sensory material of which I was not aware a moment ago. It is given as a survival, if not an encore; and to recognize it as either is to *refer* it backward to a prior moment of existence which is not the "now." If this were not so, the psychologists would have no justification for speaking of the phenomenon as a mode of memory. In every moment of consciousness which has any temporal character whatever, three components are present: first, some especially vivid content, usually sensory or affective, which *feels* "new," and thus serves to identify the moment as "now"; second, imagery, vague or clear, or fading sense-content, which is *not* felt as simply "new"; and, third—implicit in this very notion of "newness"—a conceived pattern or *schema* of relations of before-and-after, in which all the other elements of content, including the "now" itself, are thought as having relative positions, or dates of existence—*i.e.*, beforeness or afterness or togetherness with respect to one another. And in this *schema* the content of the "now" is present as *just* present, as that of which I am immediately and indubitably aware; while a part of that same content, for example, the imagery, is recognized as re-presented or pre-presented; it *signifies* events or existents which are not "now," but past or future—which have been or perhaps will be, but of which I cannot in the same sense say that they now are. Even if it be said that I still "hear" the first notes of the melody when the last is sounding, I hear them *as* past, as having existed in experience when the last note did not exist, and as not existing in the way in which that note does, at this instant, exist.

This means that any *particular* item of experience which can truly be called past, relatively to any given now, is never experienced as present *in propria persona* in that same now. The notion that it can be so experienced seems to rest at bottom upon a confusion of particulars with universals—of existence with essence. The same *essence* may, no doubt, be an object for awareness, or contemplation, through a series of continuously successive moments. If, meanwhile, there is no experienced change of content whatever—if the *kind* of thing that I am perceiving or thinking of, together with all the concomitant visceral sensations, feelings, *etc.*, remains absolutely the same—then no experience of either succession or duration occurs; the so-called "moments" are moments only in physical or clock time, not in "psychological time." But whenever any new content supervenes, and therewith a new "now" is recognized, another particular existent is born into the world, namely, a moment or pulse of experience, its particularity consisting in its having temporal limits and a relative date as after (or before) another such existent; for essences as such have by definition no dates. It is only to particulars that the terms past, present, and future have any relevance at all. And to play fast and loose with these terms, when speaking of *one and the same particular—i.e.,* to say that a particular specified as past with respect to another specified as present, is also compresent *with* the latter—is manifestly to falsify the fact of experience by a "defective," *i.e.,* a contradictory, formulation of it. This *is* "repugnant to the very essence of language" simply because it is repugnant to the very essence, not only of intelligible discourse, but of coherent thought.

But even if the criticisms of Bergson's account of "duration" which I have been expressing should be invalid, and his report of the nature of the perception of a melody be accepted as correct—and intelligible —another question suggests itself. *Why* should this subjective phenomenon of perceiving a melody be regarded not only as the key to metaphysical knowledge, but as exemplifying the supreme "satisfaction" which philosophy can furnish us? For it is to be remembered that Bergson's account purports to be merely a description of what anybody's experience when perceiving a melody actually is, or at all events can be, if he will but keep his mind free from irrelevant visual imagery while listening. Is this everyday experience so potent and precious a thing as to justify the rhapsodical language which I have previously quoted? The answer to the question seems to be that our ordinary perceptions of melody are for Bergson merely small-scale models of what it is to "see things *sub specie durationis*," but are not the full realization of that beatific vision. In such perceptions (as Bergson describes them) we find at least a little of our past experience made "indivisibly" one with the present, but obviously only a very little—the few notes which preceded the last one. But we attain the true metaphysical intuition, that is to say, "resume possession of ourselves as we really are," only in "a present moment . . . which we can dilate *infinitely* towards the past"—a moment which would thus be "the concentration of *all* duration," and therefore "eternity." Since it is not suggested that in perceiving a melody we even approximate any such achievement, Bergson's attempt at an introspective analysis of that phenomenon, even if successful, would still fail to point out to us any phase of experience open to us mortals in which the self is truly intuited as eternal. For that we should have, at best, to turn again to the hypothetical experience of instantaneous total recall. That no such experience has been shown to occur, I have already observed; but let us now assume that it might occur, and seek to understand, if possible, why even a literal and total incorporation of all past experience in a present moment is regarded by Bergson as so inexpressibly valuable.

The principal difficulty in answering this question lies in the character of Bergson's conception of "eternity" which has some obscure foreshadowings in

Schelling and Coleridge. It is, we have seen, apparently a *one-way* eternity, a "concentration" or *perfecta possessio* all at once of the life that has been but not of the life that is to be. Now, the nature of the values, the emotional satisfactions, which have been felt by men in many ages to attach to the idea of eternity are not unfamiliar nor psychologically unintelligible; but it is not easy to see how these satisfactions could be furnished by the idea of a unilateral or (if we may so express it) merely retrospective eternity. In its relation to the emotions, the eternal has usually been the refuge of the tired or the disillusioned; the thought of it, or the conceived identification of one's own being with it, has brought relief from the weariness of an endlessly renewed outreach of desire and endeavor after ends which, being themselves subject to the tooth of time, the all-devourer, cannot lastingly satisfy, even if attained. It has, in short, provided an emancipation from the anxious restlessness of the will, by making what is happening in the present or to happen in the future seem unimportant and valueless. "Time," says Aldous Huxley's mystical philosopher, "is evil" because "time and craving—craving and time—[are] two aspects of the same thing. . . . The feeling [of eternity] is a non-personal experience of timeless peace." Opposed to this "are all personal feelings evoked by temporal situations, and characterized by a sense of excitement. . . . Being obsessed with time and our egos we are forever craving and worrying. But nothing [the mystical philosopher somewhat anticlimactically adds] impairs the normal functioning of the organism like craving and worrying."[1]

Here, patently, the "experience of timeless peace" is valued because it is an escape from every form of emotional preoccupation with the future; it is taking no thought for the morrow, since, outside of time, there is no morrow. Eternity, for Huxley, is apparently just timelessness in the abstract, not an eternity which comprehends the content of time. But also when it is conceived in the latter sense, it is still usually its effect in freeing the mind of the sense of strain in the present and of the vexing unattainedness of the future that constitutes the value of the idea—the assurance (which we have seen Novalis expressing) that one's own self—or alternatively, as such idealists of another fashion as Bosanquet, Bradley, and Royce asserted, that the Absolute, that is to say, the universe —is now and forever at the goal, be the vicissitudes and seeming frustrations of time what they may. But no such assurance would seem to be derivable from the conception of an "eternity" which—supposing it

[1] *After Many a Summer Dies the Swan* (1939), pp. 117–35 and *passim*.

to be capable of being experienced—would be only an *omnium-gatherum* of antecedent existences, and would not embrace what, in the temporal order, is called the future. It may perhaps be supposed that the value which Bergson ascribes to the experience of a retrospective eternity is due to an oversight—that he has simply read into the notion of a "concentration" of all past duration the practical or emotional implications of the historic conception of genuine or complete eternity. This, however, would, I think, be a mistake. The unilateral character of Bergson's eternity is symptomatic of a highly characteristic feature of his philosophy. He was—if I may put it so—not interested in the thought of an eternity which would rob the present of its poignancy and the future of its absolute futurity. The present moment is "that which is acting," while the past is "that which acts no longer"; or rather, the pure present "is the continuous progress of the past which gnaws into the future, and which swells as it advances."[2] And it is with movement, change, the perpetual pushing-forward of life into new moments and new forms, the *élan vital*—in a word, with becoming—that his thought is most characteristically preoccupied; "that continuity of becoming," he writes in *Matter and Memory*, "which is reality itself." It would be repugnant to the temper of

[2] *Creative Evolution* (London, 1910), p. 4.

such a philosophy to turn away from "temporal situations, characterized by a sense of excitement," to a "timeless peace," still more, to admit that the world-process, when truly understood, is and always has been already consummated. If the concept of eternity is to find any place in this philosophy, it can be applied *only* to the completed past; to the living present, which is living because it is moving into a future still to be created, that concept can have no relevance.

# Index

203